**CARLO MARIA MARTINI
BIBLICAL MEDITATIONS**

CARLO MARIA MARTINI

STEPHEN

SERVANT AND WITNESS

Published in Australia by
Coventry Press
www.coventrypress.com.au
33 Scoresby Road Bayswater VIC 3153
an imprint of Freedom Publishing Books
www.freedompublishingbooks.com.au

ISBN 9780648323389

English translation copyright © Coventry Press 2019

This volume was published for the first time
by Centro Ambrosiano Edizioni, Milan 1988.

All rights reserved. Other than for the purposes and subject to the conditions prescribed under the *Copyright Act*, no part of this publication may be reproduced, stored in a retrieval system, or transmitted in any form or by any means, electronic, mechanical, photocopying, recording or otherwise, without the prior permission of the publisher.

Scripture quotations are from the New Revised Standard Version Bible: Anglicised Catholic Edition, copyright © 1989, 1993, 1995 the Division of Christian Education of the National Council of the Churches of Christ in the United States of America.

Catalogue-in-Publication entry is available from the National Library of Australia http://catalogue.nla.gov.au

Printed in Australia by Brougham Press

An Invitation		9
Introduction		11
1	TRUE KNOWLEDGE OF GOD	19
	Stephen's God	21
	Stephen as a witness through what he does	24
	Stephen as a witness through what he says	27
2	THE LACK OF KNOWLEDGE OF GOD	31
	Who was Stephen?	31
	Stephen's mentality or hardness of heart	34
	The obedient heart	43
3	THE CALL TO SERVICE	47
	Stephen's first call to serve (Acts 6:1-6)	48
	The risk of service (Luke 10:38-42)	51
	The mystery of service (Mark 6:30-44)	54
	Contemplation of the heart of Christ	57
4	THE SERVICE OF THE WORD	59
	The service of the Word	59
	Description of Stephen	65
5	THE WORD DISPUTED	73
	Accusations made against Stephen (Acts 6:8-14)	73
	Fear and Stephen's choice	78
	The service of the Word in the ministry of reconciliation	82

6	ABRAHAM, A SOLITARY FIGURE	87
	The figure of Abraham in Stephen's address	89
	Celibacy and solitude	93
	Conclusion	98
7	JOSEPH: PASTORAL FELLOWSHIP	99
	Christological reading	100
	Personalised reading	102
	An ecclesial reading: pastoral fellowship	102
	Conclusion	107
8	PURIFICATION OF THE SACRAMENTAL ECONOMY	109
	The risk of the sacramental economy	111
	Corruption of the sacramental economy	114
	Purification of the sacramental economy	115
	Practical questions	117
9	REVERENCE, OBEDIENCE, PASTORAL CHARITY	121
	Reverence and obedience	121
	Pastoral charity	130
10	STEPHEN'S PRAYER AND OUR PRAYER	133
	Who is praying?	134
	In what situation does Stephen pray?	137
	What does Stephen ask for?	138

AN INVITATION

These beautiful reflections on Stephen, servant and witness, come to us from the voice of Martini. The Archbishop of Milan made Stephen the subject of a retreat he preached in 1981 to candidates for the diaconate. Published initially by the *Centro Ambrosiano* for documentation and religious studies, these reflections are now offered once more in all their freshness.

Martini approaches the figure of Stephen from what we know about him from Chapters 6 to 8 of the *Acts of the Apostles*, 'an impressive document of a man's retrospective view in the face of death, of himself, the history of salvation, of what Christ has meant for him and the future to which he has been called.' The gain from reflecting on this figure of the martyr is tangible, and it is so for the whole community of believers: with Stephen, in fact, 'the Church feels the seriousness of being both witness and servant; it understands that abandoning oneself to God does not save one from death, but it does allow one to pass through death, contemplating the glory of God; it recognises what it is that God saves us and does not save us from and what he prepares us for.'

The richness of these meditations lies in this summary of things. It lies in the experience of a man who is approaching the revelation of the proximity of a transcendent and immanent God, and at the same time arrives 'at the culmination of his mission as servant witness,' experiencing the mystery that he proclaims, contemplates and adores, in his very own body.

God is experienced through Stephen in an 'existential contact, through which death itself takes on another face.' It is revelation, we say, but a new revelation: the docility of the heart of a witness lies in 'believing in mercy without limits, beyond immediate evidence,' and having a 'correct' awareness of such. At an historical moment when the ideological 'flag' of martyrdom is far too often synonymous with aggression, Stephen's example opens up ways to mercy as truth of being, and gift: of a being that gives of itself and a gift that is received, and vice versa, in an endless virtuous circle.

The truth of service comes from this circularity, joined with the diaconate *of the table and the Word.* Martini grasps hold of the nuances of this with finesse, applying them to the difficulties of priestly life. But even beyond the specifics of the ordained ministry, it is not difficult to see in this the features of service that can – that must – risk the challenge of opposition, rejection, solitariness. For Stephen, for everyone, for the Church, it is a service enlightened by prayer, hope, apostolic courage in giving oneself to other human beings in order to regain life in God.

Giuseppe Mazza

INTRODUCTION

Lord God, our Father, we thank you for having called us to experience the Word together. We thank you for the gift of the Spirit you promise to each of us, so that this Word may be alive in our hearts. We thank you for the gift of service of your Son, to which you call us. See, O Lord, the hardness of our heart, the burden of our flesh, the difficulty of everything that can hinder us from seizing upon your Word. Destroy in us what is in opposition to you, so that through the intercession of Mary, your Son Jesus may reign in us, who lives and reigns with you in the unity of the Holy Spirit, forever and ever. Amen.

This evening, by way of introduction to these days of spiritual retreat, I would first of all like to tell you something about myself; then something about you; something about the theme of our meditations; something about the Spirit of God that is active in each of us.

1. *Why am I here?* Some could ask how come the Archbishop, who has so many urgent pastoral tasks, leaves them aside to take up work that belongs to preachers. And it is not so easy for me to reply to such a question, perhaps because behind any choice lie reflections that are not

completely objective. I felt urged by a very profound desire that I do not know how to explain.

Nevertheless, I believe the fundamental reason – one I felt to be far more important than the urgent matters awaiting me – is the need to communicate God's word together, with future deacons. Together, with future priests.

So I came here to be in the service of the Word, and in a listening and intercessory service.

– *Service of the Word*. I will try to read some passages of Scripture with you, to grasp their significance for this preparation for the diaconate common to all of us as a shared responsibility – of yours, mine, the Diocese.

– *Service of listening*. In the time available, I will gladly listen to any of you who wish to speak with me. We will also have some community gatherings of an evening.

– *Service of intercession*. I will pray for each of you in a special way, trying to imitate Paul who prayed, not only intensely but also joyfully. Indeed, I am struck by his words when he wrote saying that he was 'constantly praying with joy in every one of my prayers for all of you' (cf. *Phil 1:4*).

How come the Apostle puts it this way? He probably wanted to say that through prayer he was entering into such a communication of hope in the glory of God 'for all of you', that he experienced joy.

This service of mine is strictly bound up with the episcopal service that God calls on me to render to you as well.

2. *Something about you*. Making a Retreat in the Seminary is a little bit risky. Unlike what happens with a football team

that likes to play 'at home', remaining home, for you, means that you do not have the emotions that go with detachment, entering the desert, that would of itself be useful as a way of placing oneself before the clarity and power of the Word.

Everything about this place is a reminder of the past, present and proximate future and can hinder the *necessary concentration* of retreat days.

So you will need to be more engaged, make a greater effort. I recall that I used to make use of a symbolic approach that is not as childish as it sounds: when my desk was cluttered with books, writings, paper, notes, and I wanted to focus on something else I used a small rug – given to me in Jerusalem – with which I covered the whole desk and everything on it. This made my room take on a different aspect and recollection became a bit easier. I believe you could do something similar.

I am inviting you to a *more extensive exercise in meditation*, to put lengthy periods aside for silent meditation as a particular experience of journeying in the world seen in the light of the Word.

3. To assist you a little on this journey with the Word, I thought I would reflect in our meditations, on the *figure of Stephen*, servant and witness.

Indeed, Stephen can easily be understood in relation to the ministry of the diaconate. But a further reason led me to choose this fascinating and mysterious individual about whose life we know almost nothing, while at the same time we know the very lengthy address he gave at the time of his death. Last September I preached a Retreat to the priests of the Diocese with the title: *The confessions of Paul*. I chose this because several times I had been in Tre Fontane in Rome in the traditional place of his martyrdom, and I spent quite some time with the final moments of the Apostle's life, wanting to understand how he would have thought back on everything he had said, written and done; the kind of dramatic summary that would have brought all these things together; the kind of judgement he would have made of himself; what, at that moment of absolute truth, would have seemed to him to be of supreme importance.

After this Retreat to the priests, I thought that we could certainly speculate on the last quarter of an hour of Paul's life, since we have documentation available, and try to re-read his letters from this concluding view of things. Then I realised we have a precise description of what one individual in the New Testament had thought, done and said in the final moments of his life: Stephen. The pages of the *Acts of the Apostles* (from Chapter 6 to the beginning of Chapter 8) are an impressive document of a man's retrospective view in the face of death, of himself, the history of salvation, of what Christ has meant for him and the future to which he has been called.

So I thought it would be interesting to reflect at length on the figure of Stephen as servant and witness, beginning with what the Bible tells us about him in his definitive experience of martyrdom.

This way we are helped to spend some time meditating on the many current situations: the Church today in its witness and martyrdom; how we are to combine service, witness and martyrdom in ourselves; the future awaiting a Church that grasps the message of the first martyr.

I do not know if I will succeed in expressing the reflections I have in mind. But what is essential is that I entrust this figure to you for your meditation. So I advise you, over the coming days, to read, then re-read Chapters 6, 7 and the first verses of Chapter 8 of *Acts*.

Stephen's name appears on two other occasions. When *Acts* recalls the persecution that came about over Stephen (*Acts 11:19*), stresses the importance of this event for the primitive mission: this persecution was, in fact, the beginning of the mission that would become a mission to the Gentiles with Paul. And then Paul had an ecstatic vision in Jerusalem, and was speaking with the Lord, reminding him that that he had stood by, while the blood 'of your witness', Stephen, was being shed (*Acts 22:20*).

Paul is linking his own past with the death of Stephen, so it should be possible for us to reflect on some of the especially autobiographical pages written by the Apostle, reading them in reference to the figure of Stephen. I am thinking especially of the first six chapters of the Second Letter to the Corinthians, where Paul speaks of himself as servant, minister, deacon.

4. The climate in which to experience this journey with the Word, the fundamental conviction that should guide us in any listening to the Scripture, is the power of the Word in us that *is the work of the Spirit.*

All we have to do is to humbly establish the conditions for the Spirit to bring the Word to life in us. Outward conditions like detachment from things, silence, contemplation, awareness of our inability to pray and to meditate.

Lord, accomplish in me the work of your Word through the gift of the Spirit. Arouse in me the ability to serve. Make of me a servant and witness. Grant, O Lord, that I may savour the beauty of your call and feel how it is for me. Grant that I may feel how beautiful it is to let everything else go to serve you and give testimony to you.

Let us call on Stephen's intercession and also Mary's. She experienced the first persecution of the Church, its first fears, the first violent death of a good man in the Church. With Stephen, in fact, the Church feels the seriousness of being both witness and servant: it understands that abandoning oneself to God does not save one from death, but it does allow one to pass through death, contemplating the glory of God; it recognises what it is that God saves us and does not save us from and what he prepares us for.

Lord, grant that we may be able to contemplate this fundamental experience for the primitive Church. Make me your servant, your witness. Grant me the grace to serve and bear witness as Stephen served and bore witness. Grant that I may share in his glory and vision, in the intuition he had of the meaning of history and his whole life in you.

This will also be my prayer for each of you over these days of Retreat.

1

TRUE KNOWLEDGE OF GOD

We would like to reflect on the Word of God as a call in our life, through the figure of Stephen. In this first meditation we are posing two fundamental questions to ourselves:

– What is God calling me to? What is the meaning of his call in my life, my personal story? Where will it lead me?

– How can I make myself suitable for my vocation? How do I identify what hinders and what helps it?

In order to reply to these, it is useful to begin with a passage from the *Acts of the Apostles* that describes the end of Stephen's life (*Acts 7:54-60*). Seven very rich verses and one of the focal points of new Testament revelation.

We can read them as a key to interpreting the figure of Stephen, because they show the extent of identification with Jesus Christ to which God had brought him. At the same time, they tell us that the consummated, perfect mission of this witness was already there, in embryonic form, from the beginning. It is, in fact, proper to the work of God to call us to something great by immediately showing us the first fruits of what will be the conclusion.

In this respect, it is a marvellous scene, full of mystery, and it helps us to get a grip on the beginnings of our journey.

It is easy to recall Stephen's words immediately prior to our text: ' You are the ones that received the law as ordained by angels, and yet you have not kept it' (*v. 53*). His discourse is violently interrupted at this point, left unfinished, cut short, yet he rounds it off in the final verses:

'When they heard these things, they became enraged and ground their teeth at Stephen. But filled with the Holy Spirit, he gazed into heaven and saw the glory of God and Jesus standing at the right hand of God. "Look," he said, "I see the heavens opened and the Son of Man standing at the right hand of God!" But they covered their ears, and with a loud shout all rushed together against him. Then they dragged him out of the city and began to stone him; and the witnesses laid their coats at the feet of a young man named Saul. While they were stoning Stephen, he prayed, "Lord Jesus, receive my spirit." Then he knelt down and cried out in a loud voice, "Lord, do not hold this sin against them." When he had said this, he died' (*7:54-60*).

I would like to identify some coordinates in the passage without commenting on them word for word. It seems to me that there are three fundamental elements on which to reflect:

1. Stephen's God. How is the God whom Stephen feels, sees and proclaims represented to us in this final moment of his mission?

2. Stephen as witness through what he does. How does Stephen embody, so to speak, his experience of God through what he does?

3. Stephen as witness through what he says.

The grace to ask for as fruit of this meditation is to gain some access to a true understanding of God:

Lord, grant that I may know you as Stephen knew you and that expresses you in my doing and saying as he expressed you; how he relived in himself the sublime knowledge you gave him of yourself.

At the beginning of the Retreat it is always important to place ourselves before a knowledge, an understanding of God that comes from him and that is not simply the result of our own thoughts and reasoning.

Stephen's God

How does Stephen grasp the presence of God in himself at the supreme moment of his death?

I would like to emphasise in particular the following words in the text:

– *'filled with the Holy Spirit'* (*v.* 55). This is the first expression of God's presence *in* Stephen.

– 'he gazed into heaven and *saw the glory of God*' (*v.* 55).

In the fullness of the divine gift filling him, he sees glory *above him*.

– He saw *'Jesus standing at the right hand of God'*, and this is immediately repeated:

'*I see the heavens opened and the Son of Man standing at the right hand of God!*' (*v.* 50).

Let us try to better understand these three indications: God in him, God above him, God by his side.

1. Stephen experiences being filled with the Holy Spirit, having God's power within him.

I would like to point out the extraordinary nature of these words, because the fullness of the Holy Spirit is characteristic of the new times. This experience does not exist in the Old Testament, only the desire for it, the prophecy: 'I will pour out my spirit on all flesh' (*Joel 2:28*).

We have here an exceptional gift of God's, the same gift that Jesus had: 'Jesus, full of the Holy Spirit ... was led ... in the wilderness' (*Lk 4:1*). For Luke the evangelist, the fullness of the Spirit is one of the great moments when we recognise the relationship between the history of humankind and the glory of God, the moment when it is made clear what direction history is taking through an inner fullness, not through an instruction.

The key to Stephen's behaviour is not found in a degree of acquired knowledge: it is the gift of a prophetic knowledge of God and of the meaning of history, in all its fullness. It is a *quid* that inserts the human being into divine action from within, such that this action becomes familiar, and that the person can express it.

So, we are talking about a fundamental grace for the witness, for the one who speaks, driven by an inner fullness. And we all know the difference between someone who repeats a lesson he has learned off by heart, due to compulsion or some outward imposition, and speaking about something because we are immersed in it.

This, then, is Stephen's first experience. God is truly within him.

2. In the fullness of the Holy Spirit, he 'saw the glory of God.'

It is a very simple line but an extraordinary one. It is enough to think of the Book of Exodus when Moses asks to see God's glory and is only given a reflection of it (*Ex 33:18-20*). No one, according to the Sacred Text, can see God's glory and stay alive.

We can also recall the prologue to John's Gospel: 'we have seen his glory, the glory as of a father's only son, full of grace and truth' (*Jn 1:14*). In this case it is glory seen indirectly, in the Word made flesh, hence made present yet also veiled by Jesus' humanity.

Stephen is given the culmination of the call that human beings can receive: the vision of glory in itself, the sublime knowledge of God beyond any human experience. In order to arrive at this, Paul considers everything else to be rubbish (cf. *Phil 3:8*).

But, we ask ourselves, what does it mean to see glory? It is clear, in the economy of the passage, that it is speaking about the glory of the Father, of the presence and power of the Father manifested to humankind. It is knowledge of the loving and merciful root of all reality, and all other knowledge derives from it. It is an inestimable gift that Stephen could never have asked for nor hoped to gain.

3. Finally, Stephen's God is Jesus – who is then called the Son of man – crucified and killed, risen, who is now at the right hand of God in the divine sphere, that is, *standing*.

As God himself, Jesus is now ready to help humanity, be with human beings, and be with them in their supreme confession of faith.

In conclusion, Stephen has an experience of the Trinity, of the closeness, the transcendence and immanence of God in history. Given that he is living within the reality he has always spoken about, he arrives at the culmination of his mission as servant witness.

In prayer we can ask: what is my knowledge of God? Is it such as to fill me within, allow me to know his transcendence beyond anything else, and also his presence in my life at every moment of my history?

We should desire Stephen's experience because it is the only one that can protect us from the atheism surrounding us and that subtly penetrates to our inner being. This atheism is made up of disregard, mentality, culture, daily gestures that assail the life of the priest, besieging him in his feelings, judgements, ways of acting and speaking. We will not be able to effectively overcome it with the power of God in us that continuously allows us to refer back to the sense of his transcendence and presence in history. Perhaps we will speak about God, show that we have a certain knowledge of him, but in concrete terms we will be acting and moving as if he did not exist, or rather, as if he were not available to humanity.

Stephen as a witness through what he does

Stephen does not only have a true experience of God, but he lives it in his body.

I ask myself: what is the circumstance in which he gains access to this sublime knowledge and understanding?

We might think it is the result of a solitary ecstasy, prolonged prayer on a mountain top, a lengthy silence lasting many days.

But this is not the case. He gains access to it in a circumstance of persecution, hatred, hardship, suffering in which he came out into the open and put it all out there, purifying his language and avoiding any hidden or indirect, parabolic way of speaking.

Stephen is surrounded by people who are enraged and grinding their teeth like a wild animal ready to attack. But he is given a flash of enlightenment at that moment, like Peter stepping out of the boat at the Lord's command and walking on the water, and he leaves any thought of prudence or political correctness behind.

It is not through his own efforts that he has acquired this extraordinary experience of God: it is given to him at the moment he puts himself out there totally.

There are some interesting indications in the text regarding the kind of embodiment Stephen gives to his sublime trinitarian knowledge: when he speaks of 'seeing' and when he 'knelt down'.

– Luke insists on the 'seeing' with three different verbs: in *v.* 55 'he *gazed* into heaven'; 'he *saw* the glory of God'; and in *v.* 56, using another Greek verb, *'Look'*. See, gaze, look. Three ways of getting us to better understand what point Stephen has arrived at: someone who sees and speaks about what he has contemplated. He is the *perfect witness*.

He gazed into the heavens and saw them *opened*. He has become a witness to the active presence of God in human history; he had the courage to understand the situation he was experiencing, in the certainty that God was close by because he is always present and at work in this world.

Jesus too, at the moment of his baptism, saw the heavens opened (cf. *Mt 3:16*).

We can certainly speak often and well of the presence of God in human affairs, but just the same, we regulate things in such a way that they find their way to safe harbour even without his help.

Stephen overcame this inborn sense of prudence, this constant temptation to atheism in working and arranging things in such a way that they do not go astray. The Church's first martyr went beyond all this and seeing the heavens opened, ultimately understood that human life has no meaning unless seen in an all-embracing way, and unless it is understood as the immanence of the living, loving God who calls, and walks through history.

– In *v. 60* Stephen kneels and cries out in a loud voice.

Eyes, legs, voice are carefully noted. It is all testimony to the event he is experiencing. The *kneeling* is not usual for the New Testament or generally in the Bible; it points to very intense prayer embodied in his outward attitude. Paul, for example, when he wants to pray in a solemn and heartfelt way for the community, says 'I bow my knees before the Father' (*Eph 3:14*). Jesus too, in Gethsemane, kneels at the moment of his supreme prayer (*Lk 22:41*), when he comes to the final invocation of his earthly existence.

Stephen experiences the presence of God in his body, and kneels in prayer and with a *loud cry*: another christological reflection – Jesus on the cross cries out loud.

God has led Stephen to be a witness to his transcendence and immanence in history, and to be so with the voice and gestures of Jesus. The witness, at the end of his life, is identified with Christ.

Stephen as a witness through what he says

The text holds a statement from Stephen and two prayers.

We have already meditated on the statement: the heavens opened, God's communication with humankind, the Lord's presence in history, the Son of man at the right hand of the Father. Jesus, crucified and glorified, is the supreme confession of faith, the Word that manifests his testimony.

We will now spend a brief moment on the two prayers: 'Lord Jesus, receive my spirit' (*v.* 59); 'Lord, do not hold this sin against them' (*v.* 60). They are Jesus' prayers on the cross. Stephen the witness, then, is the one who speaks just as Jesus did, both addressing himself to God – to whom he has entrusted himself in complete abandonment while already savouring the bitter taste of a harsh and atrocious death by stoning – and through the attitude Jesus showed of forgiveness and mercy for humankind.

He has entered fully into God's *hésed*, into his infinite mercy for each of us; he has become the perfect witness manifesting who God is, through his voice and behaviour.

It may seem easy in words, but as soon as we try to put all this into practice we see that it disturbs the balance of conflict that human beings are used to by now and breaks the habits of opposition and conflict. Here too, with a gesture that is absolutely outside the evidence and the obvious, Stephen, instead, asks God not to hold this sin against them.

From the point of view of justice and order his behaviour seems to be exaggerated, but I begin to think of other similar situations where, thanks be to God, certain individuals have experienced Stephen's attitude. I remember the prayer of Vittorio Bachelet's son at his funeral; I recall the prayer of the daughter of the Director of Health at the Polyclinic who had also been murdered, and it did not seem true that a 15-year-old girl could speak of the serene relationship between life and death.

Stephen, then, is the perfect witness in what he says at the moment of death. Indeed, it would be interesting to compare these very meek words of his with the very violent ones hurled at him; there was a journey of growth in him, and his earlier testimony, expressed more harshly, should be understood by linking it with this final one expressed in words of forgiveness. It is God who has taken hold of him from within and identified him with Jesus.

Lord, where are you leading me? What is the vocation to which you are calling me and how do you want me to be a witness? Lord, what is lacking so that I may be your witness until the end?

Let us try to reflect, personally, on these aspects of Stephen's testimony that seem more important for us, and let us ask ourselves which of them we feel we are still far from.

2

THE LACK OF KNOWLEDGE OF GOD

We have seen that the point of arrival for Stephen's journey is that ineffable experience of God, of his presence in the life of human beings and history that Paul speaks about when he says that he regards everything as rubbish in order to arrive at the 'surpassing value of knowing Christ Jesus my Lord' (*Phil 3:8*).

While we continue to keep our gaze firmly on the gift that makes us perfect witnesses, we would now like to ask ourselves about Stephen's point of departure.

– Who was Stephen?
– Where did he come from? What mindset had he been converted from?

Who was Stephen?

We find no exhaustive reply to this question in the Bible, so scholars have put forward many hypotheses. Some say that he came from the Samaritan community, and that his speech represents a piece of Samaritan theology translated into Christian terms, given the invective against the temple in Jerusalem. Others have suggested the hypothesis that Stephen came from the community of Essenes, or Qumran, and then converted, and they analyse his speech in Chapter 7 from this point of view. Indeed, they make him an observant Jew, follower of James, brother of Jesus, head of the Jerusalem community. Some have imagined that in fact his address was James' address and that James had been killed by Paul (a version that finds acceptance in the Pseudo-Clementine literature in the centuries that followed; Luke had hidden this crime, replacing James with Stephen).

Despite there being some lack of clarity about his origins, it seems to me that we can find out some information from the texts.

Meanwhile, he was probably a *Hellenist*, coming from a family of Greek upbringing. His name is Greek; he is first mentioned in the company of the 'seven' along with Philip, Prochorus, Nicanor, Timon, Parmenas, and Nicolaus (*Acts 6:5*). Nicolaus is clearly called a 'proselyte of Antioch', a Greek, therefore, who had approached Jewish practices and then converted to Christianity.

We can suppose that Stephen was *Jewish by birth* (he is distinct from Nicolaus the proselyte from Antioch) but of a Greek setting, mentality and culture. He read the Bible in Greek and had a breadth of considerable cultural baggage; he did not belong to a community with a narrow outlook but came from a somewhat cosmopolitan world, as was the Jewish world experienced within a Greek setting.

– Another reason for thinking he is a Hellenist is found in Chapter 7 of *Acts* where the Hellenists are mentioned as being separate from the Jews who spoke in Aramaic and read their Scriptures in Hebrew. The two groups are at odds over distribution of food, and so it is probably that the group of 'seven' had been set up to give a degree of autonomy and regulation to the Hellenist side of the first community in Jerusalem. We are talking about a rearrangement of things in Jerusalem involving some compromise, in the sense that a group has been given a minimum of self-sufficiency, always under the guidance of the apostles.

– So, Stephen is a man of Greek culture, though Jewish by birth, and he is *very much respected* in Jerusalem. Devout men buried him 'and made loud lamentation over him' (*Acts 8:2*). The mention of 'devout men' alludes to the observant community of Jerusalem and this means that he was known and respected by the Jews, not by the fanatics who violently murdered him, but by those who belonged to the right-thinking part of the community.

– Luke presents him to us as someone *who knew his Scripture*, someone who spoke with constant reference to the Bible.

– Perhaps there is a further characteristic of Stephen's: he had a thorough knowledge of the weaknesses of religious and intellectual circles in Jerusalem. We can deduce this from the frankness with which he denounces them (cf. *Acts 7:51-53*). Only someone who knows the people around him well can reproach them safely without being contradicted. Stephen probably *moved* in these *religious and intellectual circles*.

From this overview, the figure of Stephen seems to be very similar to Paul's. The Apostle, too, was well instructed in the Law, came from a Hellenist environment, was respected, bold, and strict. Perhaps Stephen belonged to the group of Jews who were still more thoroughly bound to their traditions yet quite militant and ready to launch into mission. Certainly, there is a difference between the placid progress of the community within Jewish boundaries – the first five chapters of Acts – and Stephen's more aggressive approach.

His friends were respectable people in terms of the religious setting as well as the civil society of the time. We should not be surprised that his death would have been a terrible shock; in some ways the city cried more over him than it did at Jesus' death. Only the disciples cried for Jesus because he was somewhat unknown, someone who came from outside. Stephen spent his life in the city and the whole city was moved by his death.

Stephen's mentality or hardness of heart

What was Stephen saved from when he joined the community and, at a certain point, took on some responsibilities – service and then evangelisation with a strong conquering flavour to it?

We have hypothesised that he came from a cultured, refined, influential world well-trained in the Law and Scripture: a world that we might call 'clerical' in inverted commas.

We note that none of the Twelve belonged to this environment, not even Matthew who was also a bit different from the others.

What was the basic vice of this 'clerical' world that Stephen denounces in his speech, with so much violence that he gives us to understand that he himself had been cast out by God? We recall that Paul, too, in his Letter to the Philippians, harshly denounces the mentality he had come from, and this offers us a comparison. We know more about the origins of the Apostle because he has told us about them, and it is symptomatic that his words become more polemical when he refers to the environment that had been his.

Let us call this mentality *hardness of heart,* so we can grasp its significance, and let us briefly analyse the *verses in Chapter 7* where Stephen reaches the height of his invective against those whom he now senses are his adversaries. We will also look at some *passages from Mark's Gospel.*

Reflecting on the question of where Stephen came from will help us understand the dangers and perhaps the death that the Lord saves each of us from.

1. 'You stiff-necked people, uncircumcised in heart and ears, you are for ever opposing the Holy Spirit, just as your ancestors used to do. Which of the prophets did your ancestors not persecute? They killed those who foretold the coming of the Righteous One, and now you have become his betrayers and murderers. You are the ones that received the law as ordained by angels, and yet you have not kept it' (*Acts 7:51-53*).

'You stiff-necked people' in the Greek text is literally 'hard-necked'. It attacks the inability to bow before the evidence and is certainly a hardening that hinders one from seeing the light.

'Uncircumcised in heart and ears' indicates, in a biblical mentality, the man who has allowed his heart to become so enveloped in hard and heavy tissue that it might as well not exist; and who has allowed his ears to become so stuffed with wax that he can no longer hear.

In fact, leaving metaphor aside, Stephen exclaims: 'You are for ever opposing the Holy Spirit.'

This dramatic indictment precisely described the *hardness of heart* that is the fundamental obstacle to the Word of God, because opposition to the Word comes from erecting this closure into a system, not just from negligence or fickleness.

2. The *evangelist Mark* offers the reader a broad reflection on *hardness of heart*. It is something that touches on us closely and not only concerns Stephen's imaginary adversaries. It is something that can even jeopardise the salvation of believers, of human beings.

Exegetes have called Chapters 6, 7 and 8 of Mark 'the Bread section' because they include two multiplications of loaves worked by Jesus and they also mention bread and yeast when the disciples are on the boat with their Master (*Mk 8:14-21*). This also gives the section Eucharistic value: the evangelist will instruct the community on how they are to treat the bread that is Christ.

These instructions are exemplified in two directions: *refusal* and *acceptance*. Refusal is developed in accordance with the theme of *hardness of heart*, the disobedient heart, the hard heart. The Greek Bible uses the term *sclerocardía*, meaning the heart has become like stone. There is the hardness of heart of the Pharisees, and there is the hardness of heart of the disciples.

a) The *hardness* of heart of the *Pharisees* can be described as distortion of the Word.

The Pharisees become the symbol of those who, having received and listened to the Word and even explained it, continue to turn it to their own advantage. Instead of submitting to the Word, they submit the Word to the defence of their own privileges, to excuse their attitudes to the offence of those who oppose them. These are characteristic of distortion of the Word, the greatest sin there is, the sin against the Holy Spirit. Stephen exclaims: 'You are for ever opposing the Holy Spirit.'

It is the sin that those who deal with the Word professionally are exposed to, and this hardness of heart can reach the level of real schizophrenia, in the sense that they know how to speak very well, can do good things, and yet there is an excruciating inner contrast with all that.

– Mark offers us some significant examples. When Jesus begins teaching in the synagogue in Nazareth, many are scandalised and he marvels at the incredulity of his fellow countrymen (*Mk 6:6*). Clearly, it is not the Pharisees we are talking about here, but people who have vested interests, who want to manipulate Jesus by fitting him into local, parochial schemes of grandeur that refuse to accept him in all humility. But Jesus cannot be understood by someone who judges him without having first listened to him, and he even feels that he is prevented from working miracles there.

– Another example is Jesus' rebuke of the Pharisees who approach him (*Mk 7:6-7*): 'Isaiah prophesied rightly about you hypocrites, as it is written, "This people honours me with their lips, but their hearts are far from me; in vain do they worship me, teaching human precepts as doctrines."' The Word of God has been gradually replaced by habits, traditions, ways of acting that have become normative and which people cannot avoid. They have been imprisoned by them.

This was Paul's experience and it was probably also Stephen's.

A kind of prison like a golden cage, because we get used to everything, because it gives us the inner privilege of an apparent security and an outer privilege of force. In certain societies it provides material, economic privileges, group honour: all things that close the heart when they become absolutes for us.

– Finally, we can quote a further passage from Mark where Jesus loses courage, so to speak: 'The Pharisees came and began to argue with him, asking him for a sign from heaven, to test him. And he sighed deeply in his spirit and said, "Why does this generation ask for a sign? Truly I tell you, no sign will be given to this generation." And he left them, and getting into the boat again, he went across to the other side' (*Mk 8:11-13*). Even physically, Jesus seems to be saying: there is no common ground, nothing we can do. The

Pharisees are actually employing a biblical theme, asking for a sign, however, they are doing this from a desire to exploit the result. Once we close ourselves to the Word, even the most beautiful words and the most moving ones do not touch the heart that is imprisoned by blind attachment to its own preconceived interests.

To sum up, the Pharisees' *hardness of heart* (considered, as I said, as a symbol) is the taking possession of the Word, not wanting to abandon what one already possesses; it is resistance to the Spirit who demands obedience instead, a neck that can bend, humility to accept what is new.

Reflecting before God with sincerity, we need to confess that we, too, are constantly tempted, more than are others, by possessiveness where the Word is concerned, wanting to make what has been given to us as a gift into an instrument of power, because our familiarity with the Word can only but recall a powerful, violent, shrewd activity of Satan's that tries to trap us. This leads to a certain rigidity of mind and life, lack of serious pastoral creativity, inability to dialogue and understand people who are distant from us, or to grasp reflections of the Spirit in the world. There are both serious and less serious temptations that come from this, but they are always harmful for the life of the Church.

Stephen puts us on our guard with his escape from this risky situation, and he invites us to consider how easily we can go from the gift received to the good possessed, and then to exploiting this good. He warns us not to become possessors of the Word, of institutions, associations, of what has been entrusted to us, and he exhorts us to be true servants and witnesses who respond to the Lord's call. But we are only servants and witnesses if we experience a profound freedom of heart.

– One further note. According to the Scripture, the energy of hardness of heart – not always evident – goes in the direction of *violence*. It seems impossible, yet Stephen connects the practice of violence with hardness of heart because, following his words: 'You are for ever opposing the Holy Spirit,' the scene moves on to persecution and murder. Stephen's opponents would never have admitted that they were murderers, but they resorted to murder once the abscess they carried within them burst.

Basically, the root of the violence of ideological opposition is also the explanation for Jesus' death. So, I believe it would also be useful to carefully explore the link between ideological possessiveness and violence.

b) *The hardness of heart of the disciples* is emphasised in the same Bread section in Mark's Gospel. The disciples are poor, they have left everything, they have been busy and despite all this they are often reproached by Jesus.

Their hardness of heart is different from that of the Pharisees, because it consists in not knowing how to draw out the consequences of the Word.

They gladly accept it, want it, love it, but they are afraid to throw themselves into it and feel some fragility.

We all have this experience of the disciples, so it is worth our while re-reading some Gospel passages.

– Immediately after the first multiplication of loaves, for example, they climb on board their boat, and during the night Jesus reaches them, walking on the water. The disciples cry out, thinking he is a ghost: 'Then he got into the boat with them and the wind ceased. And they were utterly astounded, for they did not understand about the loaves, but their hearts were hardened' (cf. *Mk 6:45-52*).

The apostles' blindness of heart is the kind of blindness of someone who has seen, has listened well, but does not draw out the consequences of this. The blockage is not upstream, the water arrives but does not flow out, does not reach the valley but just eddies around.

It is also so often the cause of so many of our moments of sadness and bitterness that become negative and defeatist judgements on things and situations. The Word is in us but it stagnates because we do not let it run. It gets slimy, filled with germs, and produces a state of mild impatience that leads to nervousness, dissatisfaction or discontent.

– Another example: the disciples are once more in their boat, but have forgotten to bring enough bread with them for everyone. Meanwhile, Jesus 'cautioned them, saying, 'Watch out – beware of the yeast of the Pharisees and the yeast of Herod.' They said to one another, 'It is because we have no bread.' And becoming aware of it, Jesus said to them, 'Why are you talking about having no bread? Do you still not perceive or understand? Are your hearts hardened? Do you have eyes, and fail to see? Do you have ears, and fail to hear? And do you not remember? When I broke the five loaves for the five thousand, how many baskets full of broken pieces did you collect?' (*Mk 8:14-21*).

Jesus earnestly reproaches his friends given that they have seen, have learned, but it has not become life for them.

– Perhaps the most dramatic representation of the hardness of heart of the disciples is given to us by Peter, the man who stands before the Word in all his generosity. After having made the most beautiful statement in his life: 'You are the Christ,' he still does not know how to submit, still does not draw out the consequences of this. In fact, when Jesus begins to teach what it means to be the Christ – the Son of man must suffer much, be rejected and driven out by those who count, be killed and rise again after three days – Peter rebukes him (cf. *Mk 8:27-33*). He experiences this duplicity, this anxiety about accepting or not accepting, understanding or not understanding.

Stephen, too, has been saved from this situation of hardness of heart and was able to achieve a total freedom of word and understanding, not only escaping from a Pharisaical kind of blindness but also the uncertainty of the disciple who is still a 'work in progress'.

Naturally, he would have put in the time to arrive at this goal; at any rate, he is full of gratitude to the Lord for bringing him out of his hardness of heart and leading him patiently through different situations.

We would also want to pray, saying: 'Where have you taken me from, Lord and where am I now in terms of hardness of heart that Paul calls *the flesh*?' The flesh, meaning the burden of the human being who is not moved totally by the Spirit and who is focused on his own interests, plans and projects. 'Lord, free me from danger and hear my voice. If you, O Lord, should mark iniquities, Lord, who could stand?'

Let us then reflect on our practical lack of consistency, on the states of sadness and dejection that are the sign of a divided heart, of a certain situation of confusion and contradiction.

The obedient heart

In the 'Bread section' in Mark's Gospel, other than the examples of disobedient, fractious hearts, we find the voice of those who have an obedient, docile heart. These are the poor, those who run to Jesus in their thousands to be healed. They do not see problems in this, and do not have the mistrust of the people from Nazareth, nor do they ask for a sign as the Pharisees did.

The mass of people who flock to Jesus in order to touch him, be in his shadow, say something to him, is made up of the poor of the kingdom, humble men and women with obedient, docile hearts (cf. *Mk 6:53-56*).

But perhaps the most beautiful image we have is the Syro-Phoenician woman (cf. *Mk 7:24-30*). She does not belong to the people of Israel, has had no instruction in the Bible nor about the Word, but following the instincts of her heart, the impulse of the Spirit speaking within her, she has immense trust in Jesus and his power. Hence, she does not give up, keeps insisting, does not take offence, does not baulk at his attitude; her heart is extremely free, therefore she can deal with her bad impression, unpopularity, and throwing herself at the Lord's feet, she repeats her request until it is heard.

This is a stunning example of the docile and obedient heart that can even struggle with God. Instead, it is typical of Pharisaical spirituality and the imperfect disciple to deal with God at a distance, with gloves on, so to speak, and set up an outer defence. The Syro-Phoenician woman is full of confidence, boldness, love. Even in the face of incomprehension she has understood who Jesus is, how Jesus is for us, and how mercy is the last word. Hardness of heart wants to talk about God's justice and human dignity – but this woman knows that the way to go is an appeal to mercy.

For further reflection in personal meditation on the obedient and docile heart, you could recall the episode with Mary at the wedding at Cana (cf. *Jn 2:1-12*): the mother wrestles with her son, confronts him, and appeals beyond his words because she has the vision of God that Stephen had come to at the height of his experience: Jesus, standing, ready to help humankind, even though appearances suggest otherwise.

It would be interesting to re-read these two female figures (the Syro-Phoenician and the Virgin Mary) in the light of Jacob wrestling with the angel (cf. *Gen 32:23-33*). Jacob had understood that God is someone you have to wrestle with, since he has to be possessed through love and not exorcised from a distance through some ideological system. God needs to be experienced through existential contact through which death itself takes on another face. This is what happened for Stephen.

Obedience, docility of heart is believing in mercy without limits, beyond immediate evidence. It means having a *correct* understanding of God.

This is grace we ask for one another, because in this grace lies the secret of being witnesses and servants.

3

THE CALL TO SERVICE

Although Stephen is never called 'deacon' in the *Acts of the Apostles*, the verb form and the noun 'service' appear several times in the description once he has been assigned the task of service.

Chapter 6 speaks about *daily distribution of food* (*diakonía*) to widows (*v. 1*); *diakonéin* at tables (*v. 2*); and, in contrast to this, *serving* (*diakonía*) *the Word* (*v. 4*).

So Stephen is correctly associated with the notion of service (*diakonía*) and called 'deacon'.

To help us to better enter into the spirit of service, the risk it involves and its mystery, I thought of two other New Testament passages: the episode of Martha and Mary in Luke's Gospel (*10:38-42*), where it says that Martha 'was distracted by her many tasks (*diakonía*)'; and the account of the first multiplication of loaves in Mark's Gospel (*6:30-44*). The apostles, in fact, have the task of looking after the feeding of the people in the desert, thus they are carrying out the request made of Stephen for the tables in Jerusalem.

We can make our reflection in the following order:

– Stephen called to serve (*Acts 6*);
– the risk of service (*Lk 10*);
– the mystery of service (*Mk 6*).

Stephen's first call to serve (Acts 6:1-6)

The reason for Stephen's call to service is a complaint, one that the Greek text calls *goggysmòs,* a muttering from the people.

– 'Now during those days, when the disciples were increasing in number, the Hellenists complained against the Hebrews because their widows were being neglected in the daily distribution of food' (*Acts 6:1*).

The departure point is a situation of hardship in the community, one that is causing bad feeling, muttering. Clearly, things were not going well even then, and they had their moments of tension and criticism.

Luke has paid some attention to the history of salvation. He uses the Greek term *goggysmòs,* which recalls a traditional activity of the people of Israel in the desert: they muttered against Moses, complained. After the triumphant victory passing through the Red Sea and the song of Moses and the Israelites (cf. *Ex 15*), the people begin to complain. 'And the people complained against Moses, saying, "What shall we drink?"' (*Ex 15:24*); 'The whole congregation of the Israelites complained against Moses and Aaron in the wilderness. The Israelites said to them, "If only we had died by the hand of the Lord in the land of Egypt, when we sat by the fleshpots and ate our fill of bread; for you have brought us out into this wilderness to kill this whole assembly with hunger"' (*Ex 16:2-3*); 'The people quarrelled with Moses, and said, "Give us water to drink"' (*Ex 17:2*).

The problem of people muttering against their pastor has very ancient biblical, Old Testament roots.

– How does the group of the Twelve react? They could have asked for patience or tried to gain time. But they prefer to intervene in a rather unexpected way. In a certain sense, they give cause for complaint but they also state a very courageous and elevated principle which goes beyond the immediate situation: 'And the twelve called together the whole community of the disciples and said, "It is not right that we should neglect the word of God in order to wait at tables"' (*Acts 6:2*).

This is *the first pastoral choice made by the Twelve*: recognising that they have created confusion by dedicating themselves to service of the tables, they remedy this by declaring that their specific service is to the Word. It is as if they are saying: it is right to be serving at table but this is not our task and it would be good for others to think about it.

Hence the institution of the Seven, in other words, the beginning of an ordering of responsibilities, coordination of levels, ministries, services. The Church saw that in order to be a well-ordered community it would have to be systematic, with clear distinction of functions.

Wanting to attribute all tasks to one person creates confusion and dissatisfaction, while distinguishing services and ministries becomes a source of tranquillity and progress for the Church.

The principle the apostles established is very important:

'Therefore, friends, select from among yourselves seven men of good standing, full of the Spirit and of wisdom, whom we may appoint to this task' (*v. 3*). We note first of all how the apostles are encouraging collaboration among the whole group. We could read into this an effort to set up a pastoral council, collaboration with the community who are invited to reflect on how they can offer service to the tables. Secondly, I am struck by a certain stress on the characteristics of those who are to be accountable for this: they have to have a good reputation – money will need to be managed – and be 'full of the Spirit and of wisdom.' It seems to us that a bit of common sense, honesty and good organisation would be enough. Instead, this diaconate has its own mystery because while it does concern material things, it also draws on the mysterious depths of the Spirit and God's wisdom.

We are beginning to grasp the mystery of service, and will return to it.

– 'We, for our part, will devote ourselves to prayer and to serving the word' (*Acts 6:4*). The apostles confirm their religious choice, almost as if to ensure that they do not let themselves be distracted for any reason from prayer and the ministry of the Word.

The episode marks not only the distinction of tasks, clarity of various responsibilities, but also the primacy of prayer and the Word in the Church. The service of tables, a service of charity, is dependent on these. The Twelve have understood that without prayer and without the ministry of the Word, there can be no genuine service of charity.

– 'What they said pleased the whole community [in our language, the people were happy that the priest was doing what a priest should] and they chose Stephen, a man full of faith and the Holy Spirit, together with Philip, Prochorus, Nicanor, Timon, Parmenas, and Nicolaus, a proselyte of Antioch' (*Acts 6:5*). What now takes place is described as a real ordination ceremony: these men step forward, answer 'present' to the call, and stand before the group of apostles 'who prayed and laid their hands on them' (cf. *Acts 6:6*).

In the fullness of their function, which is prayer, the apostles lay their hands on them and this order is established.

The risk of service (Luke 10:38-42)

After having considered the call to service, we would like to reflect on the risk of the diaconate.

Obviously, we can think of all the material services offered to the community: the tables, the sick, various structures etc.

Unlike the diaconate of the Word, these all have an immediate result. If I put up a building and see it rising higher, brick by brick, I gain some satisfaction from seeing this. When I do the budget and I see that everything is square and there are not too many liabilities I am happy, because I can then plan new work, new projects. When the youngsters entrusted to me are having fun playing basketball or football, I am content.

Martha was content preparing dinner for Jesus: she saw the meat boiling in the pot, could smell the fresh bread from the oven and wanted hers to be the best of all the meals that had been prepared for the Lord. So she was very busy with all the things that had to be done to make this happen. People from the East usually eat little but when it comes to a big celebration they can be quite inventive, because the meal lasts for hours and needs to be full of all God's good things.

What happens to Martha? Her enjoyment becomes frantic, all about self-satisfaction, and comes to the point where she is in charge of everything and decides what Jesus has to do. This growth in self-importance that takes place through her exceptional organisation in the kitchen, leads her to think that the Lord is making a mistake: 'Lord, do you not care that my sister has left me to do all the work by myself? Tell her then to help me' (*Lk 10:40*). I would like to note the fact that she has good will, a spirit of sacrifice, humility, generosity and so was not really comfortable standing over a hot oven for hours while her sister was calmly sitting down.

Martha's mistake is to think that her service was fundamental, the opposite to what the apostles had stated: 'It is not right that we should neglect the word of God in order to wait at tables' (*Acts 6:2*).

Martha believes it is only right that Mary should get up and start serving and that Jesus should not be proclaiming the Word. Her values have clearly been upended.

Service always carries this risk: possessing a value, doing something pleasing can be a substitute for what is essential, at the expense of prayer and the Word.

It is easy to fall into this error because if the Twelve had decided to solemnly establish the deacons, it means that they very much valued service – but within an order of things that needs to be observed.

Basically, Martha has arrived at a knowledge of God and Jesus that was not a true one. One could even say that this gospel episode is full of humour, showing us that even in the small kingdom of the kitchen there lies the possibility of misunderstanding the kingdom of God itself!

Only one thing matters to Jesus: the kingdom, God's good news for humankind. But Martha thought a good dinner would be of more interest to him!

The invitation to us is never to lose our sense of proportion, the sense of the Word's primacy. We can join Mary at Jesus' feet, praying:

Lord, grant that we may have the correct sense of things! Grant us the sense of what is necessary, so we are not caught up in things and worried by having too much to do.

Commitment to what we see as having immediate results is inevitably attractive to us because it is easier and can be planned. Instead, commitment to the one thing necessary is an appeal to human freedom and we do not see the immediate results. In fact, dialogue with the other's freedom replicates the outcome of the parable of the sower where much of the soil does not respond or responds only minimally; the sower would prefer to make flour soon, scorning and disregarding the time needed for the sowing.

The mystery of service (Mark 6:30-44)

Let us reflect, finally, on the mystery of service in the light of a text from Mark's Gospel.

– After having accomplished the mission Jesus gave them, 'The apostles gathered around Jesus, and told him all that they had done and taught. He said to them, "Come away to a deserted place all by yourselves and rest a while"' (*Mk 6:30-31*). The verbs in Greek are: 'gather around' – like chickens around the mother hen – and 'announced to him'. So, the Twelve return full of enthusiasm for the services of the Word they have accomplished, such as healing the sick. But Jesus appears to snub their enthusiasm and invites them to take some rest.

The Lord seeks to scale back the apostles' frantic activity that they are boasting of.

– So they leave, because they could not remain there, given that there was a huge crowd and they had no time even to eat. They hop aboard a boat and head for a deserted place. But the crowd sees them go, word gets around and people run from all the towns around and get there before them (cf. *vv. 32-33*).

– 'As he went ashore, he saw a great crowd; and he had compassion for them, because they were like sheep without a shepherd; and he began to teach them many things' (*v. 34*). The Twelve are certainly disappointed, but Jesus isn't. Basically, he would have had time to take the apostles aside and give them some advice on the frantic activity they had accomplished, but he prefers to give them a practical example. First of all, we need to note that Jesus *had compassion*, letting us see that mercy is the root of everything he does. The Twelve can grasp that the origin of their activity must be inner compassion, compassion for humanity, love. It is not the results to be achieved that are important.

Even the possibility of teaching comes from compassion and from loving knowledge of the flock.

– Then Jesus continues to instruct them, allowing them to discover the people's needs: it is getting late and the apostles can see that the situation is causing hardship.

Perhaps there is some muttering going on among the crowd, some bad feelings: some are tired of listening and are worried, since they do not know what will happen. The apostles become spokespersons for the people and say: '"This is a deserted place, and the hour is now very late; send them away so that they may go into the surrounding country and villages and buy something for themselves to eat." But he answered them, "You give them something to eat"' (*vv.35-37*). Jesus' reply is unexpected and the apostles are caught off guard.

Actually, the Lord is only anticipating what the Twelve will tell Stephen and the others: you be deacons, dedicate yourselves to the service of the tables, you do something about it. So even Jesus considers the service of the tables to be important, a service, as we have said, that was the first service Moses rendered to the people of Israel.

The passages about the people's complaints in the desert (*Ex 15; 16; 17*) also show us the importance of the corporal ministry that Moses did. After the great day when they passed through the Red Sea, something that had magnified God's power and also Moses' faith to some extent, he had imagined himself to be a great charismatic leader of the community, and that he needed to carry out marvellous cultic, religious services for the life of the people. But in fact, the people's complaints brought him back down from the heights of the service of the Word to the more immediate service of bread and water.

Something of the kind happens for the apostles who hear Jesus' reply: 'You give them something to eat,' you look after this need, don't avoid it.

– On the other hand, they experience all their limitations in obeying this command from the Lord: What will we do? With just two hundred denarii do we go and buy bread for everyone? (*v. 37*).

Then Jesus gradually re-educates them to the primacy of the Word. After they have ascertained that there are five loaves of bread and two fishes, he tells them to have the people seated in groups. In Mark's language, they become the officers and distributors of the table set by Jesus, because this service – an image of the Eucharistic table – is truly a worthy manifestation of his merciful power (cf. *vv. 38-44*).

Contemplation of the heart of Christ

Again, the apostles receive a teaching about the primacy of knowing God's mercy. They go from one experience to the other, from that of immediate service to the need for silence and recollection with Jesus; from the experience of the urgent needs of the people to that of trusting totally in the Lord's merciful power.

We, too, live amid a multiplicity of services, and we can be stretched, torn apart by all these different things, caught between the diaconate of the table and the diaconate of prayer and the Word. Yet what counts is having a right sense of values, knowing that the fundamental service is the one of prayer and the Word, and that the departure point for everything is the divine mercy to be expressed in every kind of service.

Without this as the reference point, the diaconate of the tables, while necessary, becomes self-affirmation, a place of power, an instrument of hardness of heart.

The grace that the Lord suggests that we ask for today is to be solicitous in serving the poor and weak with humility, detachment, valuing the different moments and values in play, respecting the primacy of prayer, the Word, mercy.

The diaconate experience shows us the urgency of so many of the material and structural needs of the people of

God. To this effect, due to the deficient structuring of the Christian community we are always deacons, at least in the current setup, and have to concern ourselves with budgets, buildings, equipment. But precisely because of this, there is even the more important need to get our values in order. This does not simply come from a good mental approach but above all from contemplation of the heart of Jesus, the origin and source of every diaconate in the Church, diaconate *of* the faith and *by* the faith. The former directly ministers the faith, while the latter, beginning with the faith, carries out the services of charity, never losing sight of the primacy and end which is the faith.

Let us pray that we may be profoundly enlightened by people like Moses, the apostles, Stephen who had this experience.

4

THE SERVICE OF THE WORD

Now we would like to reflect on Stephen as *servant of the Word*. While exegetes have always noted that he was ordained for the diaconate of the tables, but then carried out a diaconate of the Word, he is an evangelist and dies as a witness.

The text in Acts brings these two services together, and *Chapter 6*, beginning from *v. 8*, speaks about the opposition Stephen attracts in his ministry of the Word. This insistence on a specific situation that should not become a determining one, has its pedagogical value. However, it needs to be placed within a broader framework: first of all, we will apply ourselves to the *positive aspect of service*, then later to *Stephen's qualifications*.

The service of the Word

This service appears in the passage in Acts which says: 'We, for our part, will devote ourselves to prayer and serving the word.' Rinaldo Fabris – who usually has a rather effective translation of the texts – gives the following version: 'It is not appropriate for us to put commitment to the Word of God aside and devote ourselves to the administration of welfare.' In the sense we have explained: this is about administering welfare matters. Then continuing, he translates *v.* 4: 'We will continue to devote ourselves to common prayer and the service of the Word.'

But what is the service of the Word? The Old Testament does not know this as a typical, technical expression. Certainly, the Word was given to the prophets, placed in Isaiah's mouth, and Ezekiel was made to eat it. Nevertheless, we do not find the term 'service'. We read this word for the first time precisely in this passage of Acts.

Perhaps Luke wants to sum up in a new and evocative way a reality already presented in his earlier work, with a taste of mystery added to it. I believe it is helpful to call to mind: the episode of the Emmaus disciples (*Lk 24:25-27*); Peter's address to the crowd in Jerusalem (*Acts 2:14 ff.*); the apostles' prayer during persecution (*Acts 4:24 ff.*).

– *The Emmaus disciples.* It is easy enough to read a specific *characteristic* of the service of the Word in this account: 'Then beginning with Moses and all the prophets, [Jesus] interpreted to them the things about himself in all the scriptures' (*Lk 24:27*).

Explaining, in the sense of interpreting. Service of the Word, then, presupposes the Risen Christ, centre of history and life; it supposes a history of salvation based on the link between that history, God's promises, and salvation coming ultimately from Jesus risen and alive in the experience of those who seek him.

So, it is not about just any word of encouragement, exhortation, but has its own logic. It aims at getting us to understand Jesus' involvement in human history, even in the humanly unacceptable mysteries of his passion and death.

The Emmaus episode allows us to see that *the service of the Word is something Jesus did in the first place, and it consists of doing what he did.*

Shortly after the explanation of the Scriptures, the two disciples would say: 'Were not our hearts burning within us while he was talking to us on the road, while he was opening the scriptures to us?' (*Lk 24:32*). The *effect* of this service is to warm hearts, offer a more comprehensive understanding, to give hope, clarify things, reorganise thinking, the mind, affections, dispel fears, shadows. The two were angry at what had happened and had bitterly resigned themselves to it. They were critical and frustrated. But little by little, all this is dissolved by the service of the Word. Then they start running back where they came from and become proclaimers of the Word.

This route of service (diaconate) of the Word, which the apostles give so much importance to, is the gospel proclamation within the framework of the history of salvation, adapted to the experience of real human beings.

– *Peter's address.* In this account, too, Luke demonstrates the nature and effect of the service of the Word.

The *nature* of it: it is the proclamation of Jesus, the Risen Lord, beginning with the charismatic experience of the Twelve shown to the people by recalling salvation history.

Peter explains the significance of the historical context by proclaiming that Jesus's Resurrection is for humankind. I leave it to you to re-read the beautiful text in Chapter 2 of Acts, from v. 14 onwards.

The *effects* are visible, especially at the end: 'Now when they heard this, they were cut to the heart and said to Peter and to the other apostles, "Brothers, what should we do?"'(*Acts 6:4*).

The service of the Word is able to transform: hearts are moved, individuals consider who they are, see the evil they have done and that it is possible to live differently; they are open to hope and ask what they must do.

– *The prayer of the apostles* is one of the very many examples that show how service of the Word and prayer are closely connected. We are struck by the fact that the Twelve say: 'We, for our part, will devote ourselves to prayer and to serving the Word' (*Acts 6:4*).

These two things are connected, and it is not only an allusion to private prayer but to leading public prayer that expresses the values of deeper investigation and service of the Word.

The public prayer that Luke hands on to us begins with affirming God the Creator (quoting the Psalms and the Book of Exodus), the opposition to the Messiah proclaimed by the Psalmist, and applying these to the persecution the apostles are experiencing.

> 'Sovereign Lord, who made the heaven and
> the earth, the sea, and everything in them, it is

you who said by the Holy Spirit through our ancestor David, your servant:

> "Why did the Gentiles rage,
>   and the peoples imagine vain things?
> The kings of the earth took their stand,
>   and the rulers have gathered together
>   against the Lord and against his Messiah."

For in this city, in fact, both Herod and Pontius Pilate, with the Gentiles and the peoples of Israel, gathered together against your holy servant Jesus, whom you anointed, to do whatever your hand and your plan had predestined to take place. And now, Lord, look at their threats, and grant to your servants to speak your word with all boldness ...' (*Acts 4:24-30*).

Prayer is also a service that enlightens the present, starting out from Scripture. Its *effect* is courage, the fullness of the Holy Spirit, boldness so they can all speak the Word.

– I think we can now better grasp the significance and importance of this service of the Word as a specific task of the Twelve whom the deacons are called to help, support, and prepare for, because it clearly presupposes a certain understanding of the history of salvation, a certain assimilation of the biblical message, and a certain cultural context.

Even when there is no explicit reference to Scripture (cf. *Acts 17:22 ff.*) Paul appeals to human expectations, and human beings' search for salvation. His service of the Word consists in working on these unconscious expectations, making them explicit so he can then proclaim Christ in that particular setting.

As we have said, Stephen shifts from the service of tables to the broader reality of the service of faith that is essential to the promotion and dignity of the call human beings have.

Reflecting on the theme of this diaconate of the Word, we would like to pray to the Lord saying: *'Make me aware of this service. Grant that I may understand what I must do in order to be ready to carry it out, and how I need to assimilate the Word in order to offer and present it, in a significant context for the people to whom I am proclaiming it!*

It is undoubtedly a very difficult service that we will never be fully practised at, and that we must renew every time circumstances change. We grow slowly in it throughout our priestly experience as proclaimers, and in understanding, perhaps by paying the price of failure, that it is neither about simple explanation nor pure exegesis of Scripture.

By saying 'We will devote ourselves to prayer and serving the word' the apostles also probably mean to say that they need to apply themselves to the task by reflecting together, tackling how they are to provide this service, just as Paul will go to Jerusalem to compare his service of the Word with that of the Twelve.

Communion in the Word for priests presupposes a communication in faith which leads us to compare among us how we carry out this essential diaconate and how we can do it better, conscious that we will never be quite up to the task, so great is the challenge of circumstances.

Personally, when I am asked to explain Scripture, I instinctively feel the need to reflect on the text a lot and on the biblical context, on the people to whom I must speak, seeking in the first instance to grasp what the Word of God is saying to me at that moment.

I recall that during the last residential Week we held in Brescia, there was lengthy discussion on preparation of the homily, and the parish priest of one very important parish told us of the need to spend at least six hours a week in proximate preparation, other than remote preparation, for the Sunday homily.

Description of Stephen

After having offered you some paths for reflecting on the *service provided*, let us consider some of the descriptions of Stephen.

– How is Stephen described? Again, in terms of *fullness*: 'full of grace and power' (*Acts 6:8*), so much so that 'they could not withstand the wisdom and the Spirit with which he spoke' (*Acts 6:10*).

We could say that he is the man whom Luke never ceases praising, if we consider that he was already 'full of the Spirit and of wisdom' with the other six (*Acts 6:3*) and 'full of faith and the Holy Spirit' (*Acts 6:5*). He was clearly very much a representative figure for the evangelist, who was keen to indicate the inner fullness with which these services were carried out and that such services lead to the fulfilment of the prophetic diaconate of the Old Testament.

For Luke, the service of the Word is the culmination of all God's prophetic activity: God himself, the Holy Spirit is present in this service. God was present in the service of the tables, a service which started from faith; he is much more so in the service of the Word.

There is a very important consequence of this: we are called upon to first of all *entrust ourselves to divine* action in the service of assistance and the service of the Word. Perhaps we do so only a little bit, throwing ourselves into the tasks with great diligence and a sense of personal responsibility; or, on the contrary (and this happens with the service of the Word) we believe we know everything and can always have something to say in whatever circumstance, without thinking about it too much.

Yet the text from Acts does not remind us of our responsibility to prepare ourselves, which I have indicated, but of our awareness that we are in God's sphere, in the sphere of the Spirit's action. When we serve the Word we are led by the Spirit, and it is not permissible for us to experience this trivially in such a way that we hinder or even wreck divine action.

The invitation is to a twofold attitude: diligent preparation – which stresses the value of the service of the Word – and fully trusting ourselves to the Spirit and to prayer.

Luke's comment that 'they could not withstand the wisdom and the Spirit with which he spoke' (*Acts 6:10*) is anticipated in his Gospel where he says that when you are brought before the courts, 'make up your minds not to prepare your defence in advance; for I will give you words and a wisdom that none of your opponents will be able to withstand or contradict' (*Lk 21:14-15*).

What Stephen is going through is a warning for us: since we receive the ministry of the Word from God, he himself will give us the strength to accomplish it. It is up to us to take note of this, but also, never to think it is our ministry, because it is the Word of God in us.

– Stephen is also described as *someone who does something*: he 'did great wonders and signs among the people' (*Acts 6:8*). I interpret *this* as the shift he makes from serving tables to the diaconate of the Word, and it is interesting to see how Scripture insists on what he *does*. In the passage from Mark we meditated on yesterday, the apostles returned from the mission and tell Jesus what they did and taught (cf. *Mk 6:30*).

Similarly, Luke goes back through his memories collected in his Gospel and says: 'I wrote about ... all that Jesus did and taught from the beginning' (*Acts 1:1*).

This emphasis on doing that we also find in the diaconate that follows is pedagogical: there is a need to begin to serve, make ourselves available and useful in the most humble things so we can then gradually move on to passing on the Word whose primacy is absolute.

Whoever pretends to communicate the Word without having passed through assistance to the poor and the sick, will never grasp the merciful value of the Word and will see it as a phenomenon of culture or prestige.

I believe this is an important warning for us, encouraging us to seriously experience the ministry of the diaconate as a diaconate of the poor and the sick, in preparation for the service of the Word.

– The most significant description offered regarding the figure of Stephen, though, is the *protest* he gives rise to. In this meditation I would like to limit myself to asking ourselves how come the author of Acts so strongly emphasises accusation, opposition, resistance and finally death. Stephen is the first servant of the Word to be killed for it.

I think I can reply by saying that Luke wanted to condense the fundamental experience that the preacher and servant of the Word is called to have. The diaconate of the Word is not a peaceful, easy thing. It is not about the teacher or professor who teaches.

Rather is it a diaconate addressed to the core of human freedom to the point where it can only but arouse violent opposition. It is a diaconate that uncovers the shadowy realm of the Accuser, the Divider, the Separator, the Enemy, the one who opposes the Word of God. This reality always accompanies the service of the Word.

There are many ways this opposition can occur, and I begin by briefly describing three of them which in my view are the main ones.

1. The most evident is verbal or physical opposition: countercharges, calumny, violence, imprisonment, death.

2. A more insidious and daily form is absence, lack of response and resonance. This is the most serious temptation for someone proclaiming the Word, because if controversy at least indicates that attention is being paid, lack of response and resonance means that the Word falls into emptiness. We can think of those who never come to church, people the parish priest never gets to speak to. This form of opposition is dramatic and can even lead the evangeliser to a feeling of bitterness, resignation, inner division.

When I talk about resonance I don't just mean a generic kind of echo but the kind of thing computer language calls feedback – the possibility, through return of data, of gradually constructing a working hypothesis. The Word demands this kind of return, this reverse nourishment:

> 'For as the rain and the snow come down
>   from heaven,
>   and do not return there until they have
>   watered the earth,
> making it bring forth and sprout,
>   giving seed to the sower and bread to the
>   eater,
> so shall my word be that goes out from my
>   mouth;
>   it shall not return to me empty'
>   *(Is 55:10-11).*

The worst opposition is aridity, indifference, coldness, abstention. Then the Word dies in our mouth or leads us to look for distractions, new forms of approach that do not lead to the heart and so are useless.

3. Finally, there is a very violent and terrible form of opposition that the service of the Word encounters, and this is the accusation that comes from within us. It is how the Accuser tries to demean us, cause our ministry to be eaten away from within. We feel that we are inconsistent because of the gap between the Word we proclaim and the life we lead; we are no longer able to grasp God's mercy in our life; the Word becomes a burden for us just as the lack of resonance in the heart of the people is a burden for us; our loneliness becomes unbearable and our frustration grows.

If we don't carefully watch this opposition within us, we will be overcome by tiredness, and in the end, even though we continue to preach because it is our duty, those who listen to us sense that our words are not convincing.

Of these three kinds of opposition to the Word, the one that Stephen experiences is certainly the most dramatic, but it is not the most deadly one nor the most daily one. The most dangerous one is around or within us and we need the Word of God to transform us and constantly nurture us.

The Word in itself, as God's power in us, as the living Word, the power of the Spirit, is the remedy for these things. It would be helpful for each one to continue to reflect on the theme in personal meditation in order to better grasp this episode about Stephen.

Let us call on the great servants of the Word in prayer, and on Mary who pondered it within herself and did not allow it to be snuffed out by disappointment or in the expectation that her Son would manifest himself, but remained patient in faith and hope. Mary is the true model of the servant of the Word, the model of those who must preserve it intact and in its integrity until the established hour. May she preserve it in our hearts despite the lack of response and resonance, despite the accusation and inner defeatism that can arise and jolt our belief.

Grant, Lord, that we may comprehend the huge opposition that the Word can encounter outside us, through direct opposition, and opposition within us in the atheist alive in each of us and who accuses the Word, seeking to constantly distract us from taking proclamation of Jesus Christ seriously.

5

THE WORD DISPUTED

We would now like to re-read and meditate on *Acts 6:8-14*. Based on the opposition Stephen experienced, we would like to understand the final moment when the human being faces up to the Word: victory over the fear of death.

Accusations made against Stephen (Acts 6:8-14)

– *v. 8:* 'Stephen ... did great wonders and signs among the people.' He made God present in history, by his way of acting he changed suffering humanity into a humanity that was serene and happy, and presented people with the signs of the Kingdom.

– *v. 9:* 'Then some of those who belonged to the synagogue of the Freedmen (as it was called), Cyrenians, Alexandrians, and others of those from Cilicia and Asia, stood up and argued with Stephen.' Some rebelled against this presence, this immanence of God in history manifested by Stephen's signs and wonders. The Greek text uses the word *anéstesan* which would translate as 'jump upon'.

Perhaps you recall the strange expression in the Second Letter of St James: 'You believe that God is one; you do well.

Even the demons believe—and shudder' (*Jas 2:19*). Even they are ready to acknowledge God's transcendence, the existence of an Absolute above all things, a point of reference for values. Opposition begins when this point of reference for values is embodied and manifests its immanence in each one's life and asks to be recognised as the sign of life for society in simple daily realities.

It is then that the human being is called to choose between two ways and that the dramatic nature of such a choice is revealed. It is then that we see the difficulty in accepting that the Word becomes incarnate within history and becomes a requirement, a promise and a stimulus for human existence.

Who were the 'Freedmen'? These were people who had been slaves, and normally gained important administrative positions in homes belonging to large families: so they were part of the lower to middle class. The text then tells us some of their geographical provenance, among which the Cyrenians and Alexandrians, people from very cultured and refined cities. They were probably rich Jews of the diaspora with a *pied-à-terre* in Jerusalem, and who helped the Jewish community with their funds. These great benefactors usually instilled a degree of reverence since they had the power to give or remove financial aid.

We know about people from Cilicia and Asia better from Paul who was also from Cilicia. His impetuosity helps us understand the inflexibility that made them stand out.

It is interesting to note that up until this moment Stephen had been devoted to the service of the tables and to healing people.

The controversy arises because his way of acting is taken to be scandalous. These people see that Stephen is interested in the poor and sick, and this disrupts their mindset. The kingdom of God, the Messiah cannot be proclaimed by serving the poor! What will become of Israel, our projects, our attempt to rebuild Jerusalem in political freedom?

Continuing Jesus' work, Stephen becomes a provocateur and undermines the idea of God that some Jews had.

– *v. 10*: 'But they could not withstand the wisdom and the Spirit with which he spoke.' After having helped the poor and the sick, Stephen feels the power to proclaim the Word with a continuity of service. The Spirit who had led him to gladly help with works of mercy is now burning within him, driving him to explain what he is doing in Christ's name.

Since they could not withstand his proclamation of the Word, the assault becomes stronger and shifts to verbal, then physical violence.

– *vv. 11-12:* 'Then they secretly instigated some men to say, "We have heard him speak blasphemous words against Moses and God." They stirred up the people as well as the elders and the scribes; then they suddenly confronted him, seized him, and brought him before the council.' Clearly, the people who had begun to oppose him were very influential, people who were hard to stand up to, and gradually the rebellion spreads.

– *vv. 13-14*: 'They set up false witnesses who said, "This man never stops saying things against this holy place and the law; for we have heard him say that this Jesus of Nazareth will destroy this place and will change the customs that Moses handed on to us."' The accusation is made specific and is threefold: Moses and the Law, God, the holy place.

This triad: law, temple, God, gives us an idea of the notion of God opposing the Word. These people did not admit of a free presence of God in history, a divine ability to reveal and manifest itself. Their experience of God was locked into their own scheme of things.

The tragic side of this opposition is that the Jewish people knew about the Lord's intervention in history better than any other people, but Stephen's opponents limit this intervention to Israel's affairs. Actually, to say that God is present in history means that he walks *with* and *in* the history of humankind, and that he can always reveal himself anew.

The sin against the Spirit is precisely the sin of someone who does not want to accept that God the Spirit gives life to the world, moves everything, is present everywhere.

Stephen, too, recognised God in Moses and the temple, but in the Moses he would speak about in his address in Chapter 7: 'This is the Moses who said to the Israelites, "God will raise up a prophet for you from your own people as he raised me up"' (*Acts 7:37*). and in the temple he sees the type and meaning of God's ultimate presence in Christ Jesus (cf. *Acts 7:47-50*).

We certainly need institutional references, but to a past that is always present in the fullness of the Spirit given to us, and in the Risen Lord who communicates himself, shows himself and guides history.

Stephen is brought before the Council, then, for this interpretation of the Word in the Spirit. He dies for this vision of who God is.

– What is at stake in the accusations of the members of the synagogue? The idea that the human being is subject to certain institutions, that he exists for these institutions. So, also at stake is the notion of the human being and his freedom.

I would briefly like to emphasise that the primacy of the human being over things and institutions is a very difficult concept to maintain clearly. It can be misunderstood, confused, just as Paul's teaching was confused and misunderstood. Basically, here we digging into the Pauline doctrine of freedom from the Law that brought the Apostle so many battles and divisions within his communities.

Because also the doctrine of freedom can become a system, an ideology, a kind of libertarianism (I can do what I want, I am free and no longer subject to law). Instead, Paul states that we are servants for *charity*, all servants called to renounce anything that would offend our brother or sister. Charity is the only fundamental law in which every other law finds its justification. Charity is the primacy of the person, both as moral subject and as the centre of reference for moral activity.

I believe it is important to reflect at length on this theme and pray about it, because only the gift of the Spirit can allow us to keep a correct vision of God and the human being in a resplendent synthesis. It does not take much to debase it by turning it into a system, a slogan, a verbal sally and reduce it to an interpretation which once again is legalistic, be it of the right or the left, fundamentalist or lax, traditionalist or progressive.

In fact, the vision of the human being seen within the framework of God's mercy is the fundamental intuition for which Stephen first, then Paul, died.

Fear and Stephen's choice

Putting ourselves now in Stephen's shoes, let us try to understand his feelings.

– *Was he afraid?* I think he was. The chilling moment for him would have been the moment he was accused. Up until then he had not had great difficulty: he was respected by the community, the most respected of the Seven, and this is well described by his biographer Luke. He could speak, had the gift of healing, dealing with the poor and the sick. He was certainly full of human warmth, a kind person, well-liked. He was gaining success and satisfaction in the kingdom of God. His was a way of sacrifice, of renunciation but also a way of self-realisation.

But once he realised he was in his enemies' power and that they were standing there devoid of any mercy, then he understood that a truly serious moment in his life had arrived and what mattered was how he would deal with it.

I would call this the chilling moment, the serious situation which reveals our intentions and which will arrive at some time or another for all of us. Cardinal Jozef Mindszenty comes to mind, for example. He was Primate of Hungary. He was an extremely generous and heroic man, even if he represented an older mentality that isolated him compared to other stances taken in the Church. What struck me in his autobiography was the firm stance he took in proclaiming what he considered to be right, and the painful martyrdom he underwent for this. The first time he was imprisoned he had been a priest for just four years. He was arrested again as a bishop and cardinal in 1948, and recounts the mistreatment he was subjected to. When one person began hitting him with sacks of sand so as not to leave a mark on him, he understood that their intention was to destroy him in his personality, and he wrote: 'At that moment I understood that the whole world had collapsed for me.' In other words, he was losing his ardour, any ability to struggle, was about to capitulate, accepting the process without any power to say anything. This is the moment when you go for broke, because you are devoid of any human hope and defence.

It is the Word of God that leads its servants to this and we should not be shocked if it gives rise to a kind of inner rebellion. The great Prophet Jeremiah, an exceptional human being, complains about his calling to proclaim the Word of God: 'Woe is me, my mother, that you ever bore me, a man of strife and contention to the whole land! ... Your words were found, and I ate them, and your words became to me a joy and the delight of my heart; for I am called by your name, O Lord, God of hosts. ...Truly, you are to me like a deceitful brook, like waters that fail' (*Jer 1510. 16. 18*).

The Prophet has come a long way, served the Lord, renounced everything, experienced loneliness, but at a certain point he rebels because he feels abandoned by the One who first gave him the impetus, enthusiasm, words. This is the experience of feeling trapped, the experience of a man facing death.

Again, we can consider what Paul writes in his Second Letter to the Corinthians: 'We do not want you to be unaware, brothers and sisters, of the affliction we experienced in Asia; for we were so utterly, unbearably crushed that we despaired of life itself. Indeed, we felt that we had received the sentence of death so that we would rely not on ourselves but on God who raises the dead' (*2 Cor 1:8-9*).

We can think of Jesus in the Garden of Gethsemane when he says he has come to a circumstance he had not foreseen. His words surprise us, but each of us, if we take the Word of God seriously, will be brought one day or other to exclaim: 'Father, if you are willing, remove this cup from me; yet, not my will but yours be done' (*Lk 22:42*).

– *What does Stephen do?* Clearly, he could have escaped, asked for a moment to rethink things. Apostasy as a solution is humanly possible and this is why Jesus warns us: 'Stay awake and pray that you may not come into the time of trial; the spirit indeed is willing, but the flesh is weak' (*Mt 26:41*); 'Satan has demanded to sift all of you like wheat, but I have prayed for you that your own faith may not fail' (*Lk 22:31-32*).

Faced with death, the human being can take refuge in desperation and refuse to accept it. Instead, Stephen chooses to put his life on the line by trusting in the love of the One who first died for him. *He chooses the Word and its risk.*

This is precisely when he is devoid of any human support at all. He utters his words in complete freedom, thus confirming Jesus' prophecy: when you are brought before the courts and have chosen the Word: 'I will give you words and a wisdom that none of your opponents will be able to withstand or contradict' (cf. *Lk 21:15*).

This is where his ultimate service begins, as we will see in the following meditations. But I would like to underline the final verse in Chapter 6 of Acts: 'And all who sat in the council looked intently at him, and they saw that his face was like the face of an angel' (*Acts 6:15*). This is a truly marvellous expression and it only appears in this passage of the New Testament! Perhaps we can find a parallel in the account of the Transfiguration (cf. *Mt 17:2; Lk 9:29*); and another in the episode where Moses comes down from the mountain, where God spoke to him and his face shone (cf. *Ex 34:29*).

By choosing to follow through on this situation and to overcome his fear of death, Stephen is by now identified with God's reality and his words reflect the Spirit within him.

Let us ask the Lord that the same Spirit may lead us down this path. No human strength can enable us to overcome the fear of death, but the power of the Risen Lord will show itself in us.

Lord, fill us with the ability to serve the Word that is so demanding. You did not fool us as we set out on this path of ours because you showed us all the potential risks. You have also told us, however, that you are not asking us to be heroes, but poor individuals who, in their poverty, would like to serve the Word to the very end, with your help.

The service of the Word in the ministry of reconciliation

Normally, this day in the Retreat is dedicated to your preparation for sacramental Confession.

I would like to briefly repeat what I have had occasion to say at other times, because we need to nurture the sacrament of Penance so we can be convincing ministers of it. For the priest it is a fundamental element of the service of the Word.

We know so well that there is disenchantment in the Church today with the frequent reception of this sacrament, with serious consequences for the penitential spirit. And yet Penance should be seen as a privileged opportunity for God's action, reconciling the world to himself in Christ, and human beings among themselves.

The suggestion I am offering you is a way of broadening our understanding of Confession, transforming it into a penitential conversation which involves three fundamental moments, based on the different meanings of the Latin word 'confessio':

Confessio laudis,
Confessio vitae,
Confessio fidei.

– *Confessio laudis* is found, for example, in the examination of conscience proposed by St Ignatius Loyola in his booklet on the *Spiritual Exercises* when he says: thank God first of all for the gifts you have received. In other words, adopt an attitude of praise, since thanksgiving comes from praise and vice versa: 'I praise and thank you, Lord, because you are who you are, because you love me, have loved me and preserved me from the pit of death, and because you have come to me in my moments of sadness, temptation, difficulty. You, Lord, despite everything, have sustained me by bringing me to this confession.'

It is about allowing our spirit to expand and breathe praise. In fact, the human being is made for praise, and human beings who do so feel much more themselves.

Liturgical music, hymns in general when we join in with them, are a privileged moment for who we are as human beings and Christians.

– The *confessio vitae* follows. Augustine, in his *Confessions*, moves from the former to this one. By *confessio vitae* I mean not only what is strictly required, the sins formally defined as such, but a confession that responds to the question: if I had to indicate what is not going well in me, things that I would prefer not to face God with, what would I point to?

Little by little, we will discover the roots of our sinfulness: a certain situation of lethargy, distaste, prolonged resentment towards other individuals or situations or institutions; or we might note some inner difficulty, an inability to pray, the burden of daily effort, moral or psychological tiredness. All this can be part of the *confessio vitae* because it reminds us of the need we have for medicine, the fact that we are sick and fragile and in need of the mercy of Christ who treats our illness, heals us inwardly in the depths of our discomfort and repugnance, our nervousness and irritation.

Through a conversation of this kind it is also possible to take up spiritual direction with another who speaks to us in God's name. Spiritual direction is an anchor of salvation in difficult situations, in moments of crisis and loneliness.

– *Confessio fidei* is the tranquil proclamation that it is not we who free ourselves from sin and its roots which we are slave to. 'Lord, we not only beg forgiveness from you but we proclaim that you can forgive us, that you are our salvation, freedom, comfort, renewed constancy, vigilance over ourselves. Grant us your mercy and everything we need to overcome the aversions in our heart, our moments of bad temper, our laziness.'

Confessio fidei also becomes an opportunity to concretise sacramental Penance in something that may be linked with the burden of the sins we experience – absolution is a true *remission* of sins, the great announcement the Risen Lord gave to his disciples: repentance and forgiveness of sins is to be proclaimed in his name to all nations (cf. *Lk 24:46*).

I think we can also understand this in a physical sense as a lifting of the burden of bad moods, intolerance, feelings of discomfort. Confession enables us to pick up from where we left off.

I invite you, then, to prepare yourselves for this exercise of sacramental Penance, in the belief that to the extent that you become Christians convinced of the need you have to nurture it, you will be priests convinced of your ministry of encouragement and proclamation of the Word that reconciles.

6

ABRAHAM, A SOLITARY FIGURE

We ask you, Lord, to come to our aid during this time of Retreat, perhaps one of the more delicate moments, because our tiredness makes itself felt and we either feel we have had enough, or are distracted by what awaits us later. Show us O Lord, your kindness, so that we may grasp the treasure that is in you, the fullness you give us and that we need to experience with detachment from everything that we feel and sense superficially. Send your Spirit, we beg you, to profoundly transform us. We ask you this, Father, through Jesus Christ Our Lord.

Indeed, I believe that each of us can go through a difficult time, and that it would be good to experience these different inner movements – tiredness, repugnance, joy, ebb and flow, hope, boredom – in prayer, because this way we will learn to steer the ship of our spirit in whatever circumstances.

What is the life of the priest if not a constant seeking to steer ourselves and others in the direction of God, despite all the disturbances and less favourable times? God, who always holds us in his hands, is the truth who remains and hovers over all troubled waters.

With this certainty, let us meditate on Stephen's address (*Acts 7:1-53*), the longest and most mysterious such speech in the New Testament. Exegetes have still not finished discovering its origin. Some maintain that it has been taken from other sources and therefore has little relationship with the context. Others, instead, attempt to frame it within the account as a whole, offering various kinds of analysis.

It is certainly not kerygmatic in the sense of Peter's and Paul's addresses; it has its own particular structure that it would not be helpful to investigate here.

I prefer to read it just as we have it in front of us, without being overly concerned about its likely prehistory.

Luke presents it as the speech of a man faced with death, when only the essential things are said. We could compare it with Jesus' words in the Upper Room (*Jn 13-17*). Or, to give a modern example, with Paul VI's words written just before he died by way of a testament, as he went back over his life.

It is an address, then, that on the one hand is a *place for truth* and on the other hand is a *place for self-awareness.*

– As a *place for truth*, Stephen sums up in it some of his fundamental intuitions, along with those of the New Testament that we have already recalled: history as the space in which God journeys, and enters through his friends to lead it toward the fulfilment of a plan whose direction is from death to life, from solitude to community, from exile to home, from disintegration to fullness. Stephen's address is a place for truth about human history in which God becomes immanent, a companion to human beings. This is a dramatic history shaken by human rejection but where this rejection is transformed into new affirmation of God.

– As a *place for self-awareness*, Stephen interprets Israel's experience with the Bible in hand, and interprets Christ's and his own experience too. A key for interpreting his address would seem to me to be precisely Stephen's experience, projected onto the background of the history of salvation. It is also a source of self-awareness: the Bible is the mirror of Stephen's diaconate experience and of all the trials he has gone through.

The figure of Abraham in Stephen's address

I propose to first of all read the address from the beginning, when Stephen speaks of God's appearance to Abraham, seeing the figure of the patriarch in terms of or as an image of his own experience. Also St Augustine, when he opened the New Testament while walking in the garden, read the page from the Letter to the Romans, thinking about himself. Stephen would have done this even more: faced with death he could not ignore his involvement in the history of salvation.

How is Abraham described in the first verses of Chapter 7? You know that the story of Abraham is quite lengthy, recounted over some ten chapters of the Book of Genesis, and includes very many episodes. So it is interesting to see what Stephen has made of it, the features of the patriarch he has spoken about: 'Brothers and fathers, listen to me. The God of glory appeared to our ancestor Abraham when he was in Mesopotamia, before he lived in Haran, and said to him, "Leave your country and your relatives and go to the land that I will show you." Then he left the country of the Chaldeans and settled in Haran. After his father died, God had him move from there to this country in which you are now living. He did not give him any of it as a heritage, not even a foot's length, but promised to give it to him as his possession and to his descendants after him, even though he had no child. And God spoke in these terms, that his descendants would be resident aliens in a country belonging to others, who would enslave them and maltreat them for four hundred years. "But I will judge the nation that they serve," said God, "and after that they shall come out and worship me in this place." Then he gave him the covenant of circumcision' (*Acts 7:2-8*).

– The analysis of the account shows up some expressions, some verbs, and the absence of others.

The *verbs included*: there is an insistence on where he 'lives', 'changing abode', 'leaving'. God appeared to Abraham before he was established or dwelt in Haran. He invites him to leave and, after he left the land of the Chaldeans, he lived in Haran. Immediately after, God had him emigrate – in the original text the verb is un-inhabit – to send him to the country where 'you are now living.'

It is interesting that God did not give Abraham any property but promised to one day give the country into his possession. Then he told him that his descendants would be resident aliens and, again, would leave.

So, Abraham is seen as being *permanently uprooted*. He has the promise of land but not the experience of it. Indeed, he experiences it always as the need to change place.

Certain expressions in the passage tend to emphasise that he is also a *loner*. Stephen quotes the verses from the Book of Genesis of the so-called call of Abraham: 'Go from your country … to the land …' (*Gen 12:1*). He does not quote the verse that follows: 'I will make you a great nation' (*v.2*).

The insistence is really on the fact that the patriarch is a loner who must above all leave, change house; he is not really like the father of a multitude.

It is true that it speaks of descendants (cf. *Acts 7:6*), but all of the events whereby Abraham has a son are only briefly recalled at the end, going immediately to Isaac, Jacob, the twelve patriarchs

Furthermore, by carefully examining the Abraham account we see that he himself complains to the Lord about the repeated promises of progeny that are not realised. He is the one called by God, the migrant, the loner, and only later will he see a glimpse of descendants in Isaac; this was a very fragile glimpse given the mentality of the time, because one could hardly expect to have posterity with only one son who, moreover, had arrived in his old age.

In this sense, then, Abraham is all hope.

– Stephen dwells on this aspect, intoning it in his address against the notion of rigid attachment to place. And indeed, he was rebuked for 'saying things against this holy place'

(*Acts 6:13*). His reply was that Abraham had been faithful to God while never having a temple and always being on the move.

The beginning of all of our religiousness – Stephen seems to be telling us – has been attachment to the Word of God, not to land; it has been the hope of a heritage without enjoying its possession.

Abraham is presented as the one who vindicates Stephen's freedom of spirit. He respects the temple but does not see it as an essential condition for salvation. It is the same position as Paul's, and then of the entire primitive Church who knew how to pray at the temple but could also do without it.

All of this is probably part of Stephen's experience as servant of the tables and of the Word. He appears to be a loner and is described only in terms of his service, not for other relationships.

Without maybe forcing the text, we can read solitariness in the description of his death and burial; he is mourned by devout men, the pious men of Jerusalem, not by relatives and friends. Any description that might tie him to family has been avoided. Stephen, at least in the biblical image, is a solitary figure, a wanderer out of love for the Word and in obedience to it.

Like Abraham, he is alone with the God of glory. So, thinking about his experience of faith and life, he begins his address by saying: 'The *God of glory* appeared to our ancestor Abraham' (*Acts 7:2*).

Abraham's is not an easy situation. He certainly does not enjoy having to be continually wandering, never feeling at home, in his own country. However, his is the profound choice of a man who had been attracted by the God of glory and regards it to be above everything else; it is a choice that proposes the highest value of the Kingdom, the precious pearl, hope against all hope so as to always be with God.

Celibacy and solitude

In the light of the figures of Abraham and Stephen, it would be useful to introduce some reflections on the relationship between celibacy and solitude.

Naturally, you already know that celibacy for the Kingdom is a great and positive thing, and also a fruitful one in the sense that it leads to spiritual fatherhood. Nevertheless, leaving aside consideration here of the rich set of values in consecrated virginity, I would like to take a step further by stressing that the choice of this state of life is acceptance of a solitude or solitariness that can often be burdensome.

First of all we can briefly reflect on the *trials or levels of solitariness we experience*:

– In the first ten or twenty years of priesthood or of consecrated life, physical solitude is what predominates, hence *control of the senses*, the flesh, sexuality understood in its bodiliness.

– In the second or third decade, what gradually emerges is an *emotional solitude*, of the heart: the fact that we do not have our own family to retire to, where we can build a little corner to take refuge in.

This solitariness of daily life is perhaps more difficult than the first kind. Sometimes it can be mitigated by forms of communication, communion, but it is still there.

– In the final decades (from 50 years of age onwards) we suffer from our *renunciation of posterity*, an old age comforted by children or grandchildren.

These three levels become more and more a part of our consciousness as we advance in age and are part of the solitariness accepted in celibacy. They should not be undervalued because they are strong experiences in the psychology of the maturing human being. Sometimes, at different times in our life, they become so strong that we are surprised by them, reminding us that the choice for the Kingdom embraces our entire life until death.

We need to recognise, then, that the decision for consecrated virginity is a total option and cannot be compensated for by others, and that humanly speaking it somewhat beggars belief.

Indeed, people do not believe very much in the possibility of remaining faithful to celibacy, just because the experience of solitariness is a very difficult one.

I feel unable to say which of the trials it brings with it is the most difficult, whether it is being in control of our senses, or our resistance to emotional solitude, or the renunciation of posterity; they are probably all difficult. On the other hand, emotional balance is never ultimately achieved, but it is constantly questioned by circumstances and events, and this means we need to always be involved in rebuilding it.

Hence, the choice of celibacy for the Kingdom is only possible in the context of very great love, a passionate ideal, unconditional dedication.

Moving on to a second reflection, we ask ourselves: *can the human being make a choice of this kind?*

It is certainly important to wonder about successfully achieving this choice with eyes wide open and not just in the enthusiasm of early adolescence.

Although the Church rightly lists the reasons for which the decision for celibacy is a reasonable one, we do need to admit that it must be made because of deep affection for the Lord.

Here, we are on very delicate ground, which is the connection between celibacy and the commitment of the priest and deacon within the Latin Church. In reference to this, it seems to me that the notion that the Church ordinarily confers diaconate and priesthood on those who have already made the choice of celibacy for the Kingdom needs to be clarified, in the sense that it does not impose it as just a condition on the side.

All of which means that what is really needed is a charism, a gift that brings a man out of himself, a leap of quality in the heart, God's grace promising to keep us in its glow, its genuineness. We, for our part, however, need to commit ourselves to preserving the outward conditions, ones that are much more demanding today than they were in the past. Hence the need for discipline of the senses, the eyes, our curiosity, reading, inner attitude; also the need to be wary of ourselves and consider our relationships seriously and maturely.

A final reflection on the relationship between solitude and communication.

Solitude, we have said, is being with 'God alone', an expression the Bible happily uses to speak about the great works of salvation: God created the universe alone, God alone is merciful, God alone knows what it means to be the source of mercy. God alone, in his trinitarian mystery, is the source of communication.

If we tread via the mystery of solitude with God – the mystery of contemplative prayer, Eucharistic adoration, personal meditation – we will gradually understand that this solitude is the mother of communication.

Because God created the universe alone, he can put all things in communication and has given them all the ability to communicate.

By entering into the heart of Christ who dies alone on the cross, we are able to share in the communicative and creative power of the Church. In our poverty, we are made capable of making humanity's deepest and most incommunicable sufferings our own; we become servants of all, servants of the profound networks of human communication, available for any confidence, any secret, any of human beings' intimate, obscure ferment.

The capacity to communicate becomes an immense joy and is the fertile nature of celibacy for the Kingdom: being able to understand each and everyone, being there for everyone not just some, trusting everyone, offering advice to those who ask for it.

This fruitfulness of celibacy that follows on from solitude with God and the crucified Christ is very great.

Nevertheless, it cannot be traded, in the sense that one does not choose celibacy for the communication that comes from it. It would be as if Jesus chose death and resurrection along with it.

It is a direct path: one accepts death and receives resurrection as a gift; one accepts solitude and receives communication. The attempt to link these two things together only leads to confusion and, at some point, compromise. It is then that we begin to accept the more suspect, ambiguous type of communication, believing it is the fruit of consecrated virginity, while instead it is a mere surrogate.

I read into this all the problem of friendships among priests, the relationship of the priest with women, and the manner of conversing and being with them. Ours is an extremely difficult and delicate world and so it would be naive of me to try to offer rules *a priori*. What is required as a clear foundation is the sincere and total acceptance of solitude at three levels: in youth, and in adulthood and old age. When, as a spontaneous result, it transforms into a capacity for communication, human beings, while remaining themselves with all their inner gifts of sensitivity and affection, achieve new and vigorous expression through it.

Conclusion

I am aware that it is not easy to express this in words. Just the same, the Lord shows it to us day by day through gradual though not always easy development. I do say, however, that today it is almost impossible to observe celibacy unless one is supported by a deep charge of life in the Spirit; it is an experience that involves us in a constant struggle until the heart is fully purified by the Lord's love.

Whoever chooses and accepts this charism as a gift, as well as needing inner discipline also needs a spiritual adviser to whom he can freely manifest the interior movements of the spirit and life's events. He will help us to experience this gift in truth; there is no greater torment than a life which is divided over this, either because one has recourse to subterfuge, a double life, or because one remains discontent and resentful at the choice one has made.

I felt it was important to offer you this reflection on the topic of priestly celibacy, in the light of the experience of Stephen, Abraham and whoever takes the Word of God and service of the Word seriously as a diaconate to which they dedicate the integrity of their being.

Grant, Lord, that we may understand the beauty of consecrated virginity and love our choice that is our response to the infinite love with which you have called us. May we journey through this life in sincerity of heart and with a joy that daily becomes an ever new and creative form of true communication with every human being.

7

JOSEPH: PASTORAL FELLOWSHIP

Continuing with our meditation on Stephen's address, I have the impression that words are ever more inadequate for expressing the joy and simplicity that the mystery carries within itself. And indeed, seeking to communicate it, we end up losing something of the profundity that is proper to the God it reveals.

So, I have decided to offer you simply a few paths in schematic fashion, and each of you can use them according to need and the inner promptings of the Spirit.

After the Abraham episode, Stephen evokes the story of Joseph, one of the longest stories in the Old Testament. What is the exegetic meaning of the summary we read in Acts (7:9-16)?

A student of mine at the Biblical Institute who was studying the text at length at the time, had an interesting intuition: he distinguished four sections in the entire address: Abraham, Joseph, Moses, the desert journey toward the temple. He saw an alternating appeal to two themes in them: one *liturgical* the other *christological*. Liturgical in Abraham, christological in Joseph;

christological in Moses; liturgical in the story of the desert and the entrance to the promised land.

These themes alternate in chiasmic fashion and are substantially Stephen's response to the two objections launched against him.

One objection concerns the temple ('This man never stops saying things against this holy place' *Acts 6:13*). Here is the liturgical theme: what does it mean to adore God and what is the temple's relationship to adoration?

The other concerns Moses ('We have heard him speak blasphemous words against Moses' *Acts 6:11*), and Stephen introduces the christological theme: will Christ change the laws given by Moses?

If the Abraham episode was a liturgical reminder – Abraham adored the glory of God while moving from place to place – the story of Joseph highlights the function of Christ.

So, I would suggest first of all a *christological* reading of the Joseph account; then a more *personalised* reading, since Stephen sees his own experience in the light of Jesus' experience; finally, an *ecclesial and personal* reading.

Christological reading

The text says:
'The patriarchs, jealous of Joseph, sold him into Egypt; but God was with him, and rescued him from all his afflictions, and enabled him to win favour and to show wisdom when he stood before Pharaoh, king of Egypt, who

appointed him ruler over Egypt and over all his household. Now there came a famine throughout Egypt and Canaan, and great suffering, and our ancestors could find no food. But when Jacob heard that there was grain in Egypt, he sent our ancestors there on their first visit. On the second visit Joseph made himself known to his brothers, and Joseph's family became known to Pharaoh. Then Joseph sent and invited his father Jacob and all his relatives to come to him, seventy-five in all; so Jacob went down to Egypt. He himself died there as well as our ancestors, and their bodies were brought back to Shechem and laid in the tomb that Abraham had bought for a sum of silver from the sons of Hamor in Shechem' (*Acts 7:9-16*).

We can clearly distinguish two parts in this passage: the first concerns Joseph betrayed by his brothers, then he is freed and becomes a great man (*vv. 9-10*). The second is the rediscovered relationship between Joseph, his father and his brothers in the story of the famine, his brothers coming as ambassadors, and the help he gave them (*vv. 11-15*).

The conclusion is in *v. 16*, already projected into the future.

– Reading it carefully, line by line, we see Christ who was also condemned out of jealousy, betrayed, but never abandoned by God who, in the end, frees him from the anguish of death and places him over his people.

– The second part, in which Joseph made himself known to his brothers and fills them with gifts, recalls aspects of Christ's life, especially Jesus who *makes himself known* to his disciples after his resurrection, and re-establishes them as companions at his table.

Stephen would appear to be saying to his listeners: Careful! You are rejecting the Christ whom God has placed over his people, the people which is for your salvation and with whom God is present.

Personalised reading

The story of Joseph, however, is also the story of Stephen who is about to be betrayed out of jealousy, who has had an experience of serving at the tables, an experience of community. He is being betrayed, but God is with him and will free him from all his trials.

Stephen reads his own situation, with immense trust, in the ancient patriarch who was rejected then exalted by God: if God did not abandon Joseph, he will not abandon me and will see that my death is a service to the brethren.

Perhaps it is precisely through this episode in the history of salvation that he understands how he has been called to identify himself with the experience of Jesus.

An ecclesial reading: pastoral fellowship

The figure of Joseph also urges us to reflect on pastoral fellowship: threatened, purified and rediscovered. These are three stages we can rediscover in each of our own stories.

1. *Pastoral fellowship threatened.* The biblical account warns us that even the best of families has its problems.

Basically, Joseph's was an exemplary family, a patriarchal one where there was uprightness, serenity, joy, work, solidarity, friendship. Naturally, even in patriarchal families there can be tensions and quarrels, including strong ones, even hatred and divisions that last for generations.

There were jealousies and divisions in Jacob's case.

– So, fellowship is not obvious and is indeed under threat, both in the Church and among ourselves. It is threatened by zeal (*zelòsantes*, in the Greek text) which is jealousy. We are always living in a situation in which the separator, the enemy of humankind, sows weeds of the most unimaginable kind. No wonder the ancients spoke of 'clerical' jealousy as something terrible, awfully harsh.

Satan is called the divider or calumniator, precisely because he insinuates mistrust, jealousy, grumbling resulting from gossip, even in jest, and from words that are repeated and magnified that poison pastoral fellowship, and communities spit into groups *pro* and *con* the parish priest.

Joseph's brothers certainly came to the point where they wanted to kill him, and this seems hardly believable. The intended murder, though, became a sale, a kind of civil death where the personality was buried in the infamy of slavery; the father was deceived; clothes were soaked in blood – these are all things that reveal the terrible inventiveness of jealousy, of resentments nurtured over years.

– Other than the threatened fellowship of priestly interrelationships, of priests with their communities and vice versa, of superiors with their subjects, we can think of relationships within families. Our ministry brings us to knowledge of the shadows, the harsh and difficult moments families go through, the crises of communication between parents and their children, the incomprehension between husband and wife, etc. These are all forms of threatened fellowship pointing to the activity of the divider among us and also the weeds growing amid humankind, always ready to sprout.

– Perhaps it is possible to explain some simple misunderstandings that have given rise to mistrust, even among saints. Anyone who reads history with a critical and impartial eye, and not simply in hagiographic terms, can easily discover the difficulties the saints experienced. Part of this is because they were not always easy individuals to live with, were imperious, or insisted on their own ideas and were not always able to understand others' points of view. The primitive Church, too, does not hide constant threats to its fellowship.

– Nevertheless, we need to pay attention to see that we do not set up little islands of refuge out of fear of possible suspicion, jealousy, grouches. This type of loneliness we force upon ourselves out of fear is very dangerous and is another kind of threat to pastoral fellowship.

2. *Pastoral fellowship purified.* Fortunately, the Joseph story offers us a second side: fellowship threatened is purified by divine providence, by the infinite love of the Lord.

– God does not abandon the just person, even if such individuals have committed faults out of naivety. Joseph gives the impression that he had been somewhat naive in telling his brothers, then his father, about his dreams. Showing that he would be the leader of everyone could only cause trouble, even more so since Jacob had shown some favouritism to him.

He needed to be purified. He had to understand, through trial, that God alone is great; that God 'was with him' (*Acts 7:9*). His support was to come not from his father's favouritism, not from his natural gifts, nor his dreams, but only from the Lord. It is clear that he began to experience God's closeness while lying in the deep well, and we can easily read reference to this situation in certain of the psalms: 'He drew me up from the desolate pit'; 'you have delivered my soul from the depths of Sheol' (cf. *Ps 40:2; 86:13*). He felt there what it means to trust in God alone, the positive meaning of being alone with God. Then this experience continues in the Egyptian prison.

Joseph is freed from his naivety, from placing too much trust in other human beings and from a childish reliance on others. It is not without reason that John the evangelist has a strange line that could sound sceptical, when he says that Jesus trusted in no one in Jerusalem because 'he himself knew what was in everyone' (*Jn 2:25*).

Our knowledge of others, which begins with knowledge of ourselves, of our jealousies and ambitions, becomes mercy, forgiveness, and great understanding when it is purified by God. Joseph moved from naivety to mercy, paying for it dearly and through the grace of the Lord who 'rescued him from all his afflictions' (*Acts 7:10*).

– The purification of Joseph's brothers is also a bitter experience for them: famine, kneeling before a foreigner, the humiliation of being accused of theft, Benjamin kept as a hostage. Though they had sinned grievously against their own blood, God loves them and purifies them, not by simply condoning the sin in a gratuitous way but by rebuilding them along the way, giving them the possibility of arriving at a third moment of fellowship after the drama of isolation and hunger.

3. *Fellowship rediscovered.* In Stephen's very brief summary, what is emphasised is Joseph's brothers' recognition of him, so fellowship (fraternity, really in this case) rediscovered, rebuilt through suffering.

Like Jesus, killed by his enemies and abandoned by his followers, once risen, he makes himself known and gives peace, so does Joseph make himself known. He exercises the diaconate of consolation for his brothers, who allow themselves to be consoled by him.

I would like each of you, in silent prayer, to think over this providential journey: through trials, separation, calumny, loneliness, God sees that fellowship is rediscovered, not just as a kind of camaraderie, but as his gift.

He is the one who rebuilt Joseph in brotherhood with his kin and regenerated the unity of that family.

Let us try to think back over our experiences: past, present, community, group, relationships with superiors, communication in the Church and the world.

Conclusion

The story of Joseph brings to mind a recollection of John XXIII. On 2 June 1963, when he died, I was in Germany and heard a comment from a Protestant on German radio, summing him up thus: 'He is the one who said: "I am Joseph your brother."'

He was the one who established a relationship with his brother bishops. He descended from the heights of a pharaoh-like pedestal, where he found Joseph in the splendour of his glory, made himself known and thus concluded a journey of fellowship.

We are encouraged to also reflect on fellowship in the Church, on the fellowship of the pope with the bishops and the bishops with their priests.

The recognition of fellowship is not something trite, or a cheap kind of democratisation. It is won at great price through effort and self-giving.

This applies to all kinds of relationships, including the one the Council asked to be established between the priest and the community through every kind of collaboration, presence, shared participation.

If we think this kind of fellowship is easy, we will fall into the temptation of obvious and natural fellowship, the source of jealousy, individualism, taking sides, political games. Instead, the Lord asks us to receive it and experience it as a gift from God, the result of a journey of purification of faith and of the death and resurrection of Christ, in whom there is no difference. Because we are all one in Christ Jesus.

8

PURIFICATION OF THE SACRAMENTAL ECONOMY

We would like to reflect on the second liturgical section of Stephen's address – the desert way to the promised land – that begins at *v. 40*.

I think it would be more useful to postpone the meditation on Moses (*Acts 7:17-39*).

v. 39 assumes that Israel, after having left Egypt, continues to disobey Moses and the Word of God. This is why he turns to Aaron:

"'Make gods for us who will lead the way for us; as for this Moses who led us out from the land of Egypt, we do not know what has happened to him." At that time they made a calf, offered a sacrifice to the idol, and revelled in the works of their hands. But God turned away from them and handed them over to worship the host of heaven, as it is written in the book of the prophets:

> "Did you offer to me slain victims and sacrifices
>   for forty years in the wilderness, O house
>   of Israel?
> No; you took along the tent of Moloch,

and the star of your god Rephan,
    the images that you made to worship;
so I will remove you beyond Babylon.'

Our ancestors had the tent of testimony in the wilderness, as God directed when he spoke to Moses, ordering him to make it according to the pattern he had seen. Our ancestors in turn brought it in with Joshua when they dispossessed the nations that God drove out before our ancestors. And it was there until the time of David' (*Acts 7:40-45*).

The passage is dense and rather confused, not easy to put into order or understand, including the way the sentences are put together. But all we want to do is to establish the basic question underlying our meditation so we can then express it through a series of reflections.

If we bear in mind that Stephen, faced with the ferocious accusations levelled at him, intends to make an audacious proclamation of God who creates history, I believe the serious question is as follows: *where is God?*

We need to recognise that this is a recurring question at different times in our life. Someone going through a trial of loneliness, suffering, abandonment, or any other special circumstance, can ask whether God is still with him and how.

For example, I remember that on the day of my entrance to Milan Archdiocese, observing the crowd in the square in front of the cathedral, I felt the question arise: Where is God? Is he beyond all this, is he transcendent, or is he in these people, immanent?

In common with his opponents, Stephen wanted to know how to find the Lord in rites, in the temple arrangements, worship, liturgy, sacrifices.

In reflecting on Abraham, we understood that he found God in his direct relationship with his glory accompanying him everywhere: in Mesopotamia, near the river, in Haran, in his various wanderings. It was the transcendent dimension of the divine that found expression in him.

But the problem remains of his immanence in history and daily reality, especially in the liturgical and sacramental economy. Stephen points out some directions for us in this passage. I suggest that you re-read the following verses in particular: 'Make gods for us who will lead the way for us' (*v. 40*); '[They] revelled in the works of their hands' (*v. 41*); 'But God turned away from them and handed them over to worship the host of heaven' (*v. 42*); 'Our ancestors had the tent of testimony in the wilderness ... Our ancestors in turn brought it in' (*vv. 44-45*).

vv. 40-41 suggest a reflection on the *risk of the sacramental economy. v. 42* suggests reflection on *possible corruption of the sacramental economy* in human hands. *vv. 44-45* propose *purification of the sacramental economy*, the correct notion of God's presence.

The risk of the sacramental economy

The Jews had actually mythologised the figure of Moses; they were too attached to him. As a consequence, when he disappeared (up the mountain), they felt they had lost everything. Hence they felt a need to have something they could see and they make their request to Aaron.

Exegetes interpret this first temptation in the desert not as idolatry true and properly speaking but as an attempt to have an image of the true God (in the strength of the bull made of melted gold and bronze).

The risk of the sacramental economy is based on an essential fundamental requirement: human beings want to see and feel God, and the sacramental economy partly responds to this desire. But it can be made into an absolute and then, while the tendency to look for God remains, we are satisfied with gestures. Liturgy takes pleasure in itself, becomes a well-ordered way of coming together to satisfy the deep emotion that symbols and absolute but undefined values seek to express.

This is a liturgical economy that is easily content with the exactness of its performance and the beauty of what we are doing. Naturally, it does not deny that there is a God beyond it, greater than it, but basically, this God is no longer so important.

This risk is not necessarily a moral aberration; it is a risky tendency that human beings are satisfied with, given that God is beyond reach and cannot be represented through images. Human beings, then, feel reassured and can thus surmount their existential anguish.

We could ask ourselves: how does God show himself in our liturgies? There is no single answer to this question because it depends on different communities. I personally have the experience that in some liturgies, the mystery of

God is very much present, and in some way they go beyond themselves. For others, instead, I have the impression that the people are not grasping the mystery and all effort is exhausted in rites and gestures.

I would like to recall here a splendid liturgy I experienced years ago at Czestochowa. A huge crowd had come from so many countries, with women wrapped in their country head scarfs, on their knees after after hour on the bare ground at the church, praying. It was very clear to me that those people were experiencing the presence of God, transcendent and immanent, among them but different from them all. I was not taking part in a simple community celebration but in a celebration of the absolute and inexpressible God. This is the energy in the sacramental economy that transcends itself in order to express God's absoluteness in history and in his people.

We need to keep watch so that the liturgical gestures we carry out, the prayers we say, are both done carefully and respectfully but that they also refer to what is always beyond, always other than themselves.

The temptation the Jews had was that they did not want to wait: to go beyond, they needed to wait for Moses and the Word. Instead, they quivered with a desire to see immediately, to celebrate, even at the cost of sacrifice, since inevitably, building the bull meant they had to give up their bracelets and rings.

The end result was the crisis that erupted between Moses who broke the tablet of the Law and the people dancing around their sacred bull to a god whom they had made to satisfy their need to see and touch.

The invitation to us is not to take our sacramental liturgical celebrations for granted, given that it is very easy to be celebrating ourselves instead of God's presence.

Corruption of the sacramental economy

– From here they shifted to consummate idolatry; and to punish them, God 'turned away from them and handed them over to worship the host of heaven' (*v. 42*) to offer their offerings and sacrifices to Moloch's tent, and hence also human sacrifice, the killing of the newborn.

This is real corruption of the sacramental economy. It continues to be religious – because idolatry is a religious act – but it has given way to human self-representation.

Earlier, the tendency was to transcendence, even though it was an effort to perceive it. In this case, it flows toward the human being as they adore themselves and their own history. It is a corruption that is immoral, where the creature adores his own vices.

As we know, through development of language and culture, idolatrous corruption becomes the adoration of money, possessions, pleasure, sex, power.

These are all things that are close to the human heart and therefore to our hearts.

– Among these possible corrupt forms of the sacramental economy I would especially like to stress not so much religious or immoral idolatry, but *idolatry of a moral and civil kind* where, by virtue of the same principle, justice, good conscience, honourableness are worshipped. These are all beautiful things and, by analogy with liturgical rites, are open to what is on high, transcendent and able to help us understand the otherness of the immanent God. But sometimes they can be experienced in closed ways: justice that is self-pleasing; good conscience that is the cult of the individual; honourableness that practically becomes the placement of ourselves at the centre of the universe; a cult of civilisation, culture, race, traditions that becomes paganism.

Cruelty, massacres, Nazi extermination camps, for example, show very well the distortion in the human heart that can provoke apparently moral forms of idolatry such as the cult of nation and duty.

It seems to me that we see here the painful image of the corruption of the sacramental economy that is basically linked to an otherwise wonderful attitude, the search, that is, that the human being makes for God, an Absolute to which he or she can give themselves. But it ends up being to the detriment of the human being.

Purification of the sacramental economy

– 'Our ancestors had the tent of testimony in the wilderness, as God directed when he spoke to Moses, ordering him to make it according to the pattern he had seen. Our ancestors in turn brought it in ...' (*vv. 44-45*).

The very humble image of the tent is the purification of the sacramental economy, the correct notion of God's presence.

A tent is something very simple, close to everyone's experience. However, it is made according to the pattern Moses had seen and therefore comes from on high. It indicates the origin from which it comes and to which it refers.

– It opens up a reflection on the mystery of the tent, because the expression: 'The *schené* of testimony' immediately reminds us of John's words: Jesus lived among us, laid out his tent, in Greek, *eskénosen* (cf. *Jn 1:14*).

Any aberration of the sacramental economy, oscillating between the extreme of indifference and the extreme of idolatry through the range of intermediate steps embraced by human existence, is corrected by God with love and mercy and brought to the correct measure which is Jesus made flesh living among us. His is a discrete way of living among us, a humble way which also points to the otherness of God, to the incomparable nature of the Kingdom, the infinite and extraordinary love of God for humankind and the closeness of such love to each human being.

The various intermediate steps of the aberration of the sacramental economy, covering all of human life, range from popular superstition to all kinds of magic, predicting the future, secret rites in certain Masonic rituals and of certain sects.

The sacramental economy is purified by Christ who sums it all up in himself. Jesus among us, veiled, proclaims the Other to us, the different, incomparable God-with-us. We can never cease to be amazed at this ineffable truth. *Mirabile mysterium! O sacrum convivium, in quo Christus sumitur!*

The synthesis of God's action with humanity and our journey towards God, of the historical immanence of God in the world and the strong leaning towards transcendence is found in the historical presence of Christ: in his life, in the Gospel, the Scriptures, in his resurrection, in the Eucharist, the Church.

The correct sacramental economy, then, is a gift given to humankind, and not the result of a balance of intelligence.

Practical questions

I would like to end with some questions that can be useful for our ministry.

– What Presence is there in our assemblies?

– Who are we celebrating? Our desire for God? Our tradition? Our faith? Or are we celebrating Christ?

– Is our sacramental economy transparent and indicative, or is it opaque and reductive?

Obviously this depends more on hearts than on signs, because it is in hearts that the sacramental economy finds its correct interpretation. However, hearts match the signs and vice versa.

The Church is certainly journeying towards the fullness of the Kingdom, and along this journey it must review and try to adapt its sacramental economy. On the other hand, the effort to adapt is one that is felt throughout the ages because it is a case of adapting the liturgical economy to the truth it signifies.

I was very much struck by a passage from St Augustine in the readings in the breviary for the feast of St Damasus – who worked actively for the veneration of the saints and martyrs in particular. The passage is from the Treatise 'against Faustus'. The great doctor explains how we honour the martyrs; the question is whether it is possible to honour them and he replies: yes, but 'the veneration strictly called "worship", or latria, that is, the special homage belonging only to the divinity, is something we give and teach others to give to God alone. The offering of a sacrifice belongs to worship in this sense (that is why those who sacrifice to idols are called idol-worshippers), and we neither make nor tell others to make any such offering to any martyr, any holy soul, or any angel. If anyone among us falls into this error, he is corrected with words of sound doctrine and must then either mend his ways or else be shunned.'

He then continues by explaining how even Paul and Barnabas fell into this error then corrected it, and he concludes: 'Yet the truths we teach are one thing, the abuses thrust upon us are another. There are commandments that we are bound to give; there are breaches of them that we are commanded to correct, but until we correct them we must of necessity put up with them.'

So Augustine felt the practical difficulty of inculcating the correct form of veneration in the people's way of acting.

This is why the question as to who we are celebrating is a useful one: Who are we celebrating in our Eucharists? Ourselves or the risen Christ, image of the invisible, transcendent God, whose Name cannot be spoken and whom no one has seen or can see?

Let us ask, through the intercession of Stephen, that the Holy Spirit teach us how to go beyond the sacramental signs to love the One who deserves to be loved unconditionally; how to fix our gaze, our attention, our heart on Jesus the Son of God, perfect image of the Father, the historical Presence of the Absolute, source of perfect love. He alone allows us to purify the service we are called to render, because there is no other historical economy other than this one, after Christ taught us its correct significance.

9

REVERENCE, OBEDIENCE, PASTORAL CHARITY

At this point, I would have liked to reflect together with you on the section on Moses, the longest part of Stephen's address (*Acts 7:17-39*), and this has a christological background.

But some of you have asked me to first of all explain the terms 'reverence and obedience' found in the question the bishop puts to ordinands during the ordination rite: 'Do you promise me and my successors reverence and obedience?'

And then to speak about 'pastoral charity' which the commitment of celibacy asked of someone who exercises the sacred ministry is the 'sign and symbol' of.

So, I am leaving the continuation of reading Stephen's address to your personal meditation, even though, by reflecting on pastoral charity, we will recover a part of the episodes of Moses described in Chapter 7 of Acts.

Reverence and obedience

While the ordinand is being asked this question, he places his hands in the bishop's hands, and this gesture is undoubtedly a symbol of an important commitment.

1. How might one re-translate the word 'reverence' into New Testament Greek? I thought of some words:

a) *Eusébeia*, or 'pietas' in Latin, is the attitude of reverence for the mystery of God and man. Of itself it is a secular virtue, even though it indicates religious and not specifically Christian people. The men who buried Stephen were *eusebéis*, because they respected God and human beings. The Gentile Cornelius, in Chapter 10 of Acts, is also called *eusebéis kaì foboùmenos ton theòn*, pious and God-fearing.

Reverence, then, is something shown by the upright, just person; in the Latin pagan tradition, *pietas* is the typical virtue that controls the affectionate and respectful relationship between husband and wife, children and their parents. We could say that it is one of the attitudes, in biblical terms, that follows on from the covenant: mutual respect comprising solidarity, attention, a sense of belonging.

In Greek, *eusébeia, fòbos, eulàbeia* are also words with profound significance in ancient religion, then taken up and harmonised with Stoicism. It is enough to consider that St Charles Borromeo was happy to read the works of the Stoics – Epictetus for example – finding spiritual nourishment there for how he lived his own life.

b) Another word comes from the verb *entrépein*, translated by the Vulgate as *vereor* and used in some significant contexts. In the parable of the wicked tenants, for example, when the landowner sends his son, after sending his servants, he says: 'They will *respect* my son,' *entrapésontai*, in Latin, *verebuntur* (*Mt 21:37*). It is another way of indicating respect for a mystery.

c) Also interesting is the negative form of this attitude in the strange figure of the unjust judge who 'neither feared God nor had respect for people' (*Lk 18:2*). He would say to himself: 'Though I have no fear of God and no respect for anyone, yet because this widow keeps bothering me, I will grant her justice, so that she may not wear me out by continually coming' (*vv. 4-5*).

Paradoxically, it points to an attitude that sums up a whole life.

d) Finally, a passage came to mind from the Letter to the Hebrews where it speaks of the relationship between a father and a son: 'Moreover, we had human parents to discipline us, and we respected them. Should we not be even more willing to be subject to the Father of spirits and live? For they disciplined us for a short time as seemed best to them, but he disciplines us for our good, in order that we may share his holiness. Now, discipline always seems painful rather than pleasant at the time, but later it yields the peaceful fruit of righteousness to those who have been trained by it' (*Heb 12:9-11*). Here, reverence finds reference to the theme of human and divine correction.

These texts help us to gain a better grasp of the relationship we call reverence. Thinking back to the meditation on Joseph and his brothers, and the one about the mystery of sacramentality, perhaps we can say that the reverence promised to the bishop is in accordance with fellowship and sacramentality.

– It is in accordance with fellowship, fraternity, since it is the mystery of recognition between Joseph and his brothers, where the relationship between brothers is reconstituted by the work of God once that is accepted. Reverence here is the sense of solidarity, belonging, family relationships re-established among them, generated by the Word of God and called by this Word to an identical ministry, service, though of varying degrees and responsibilities.

– It is in accordance with sacramentality, since reverence means recognising that the mystery of Christ, which gives order to our life, passes sacramentally through people, figures, symbols.

This assumes we have genuflected before the mystery of God and his revelation of himself in history: in Christ, the Church, individuals. Here we need to have a biblical, historical, christological faith to which we respond in freedom, just as God's action in history is free.

2. The mystery contained in reverence is further specified by *obedience*.

In the New Testament this is easily expressed by the Greek verb *up-akoùein* literally translated into Latin as *ob-audire*.

This refers to 'listening with submission', a reverent and prompt way of listening.

One of the basic reference texts for understanding what 'I promise obedience' means is in the Letter to the Romans:

'For just as by the one man's disobedience [in Greek, *parakoè*, to listen then ignore] the many were made sinners, so by the one man's obedience [in Greek, *upakoè*, submissive listening] the many will be made righteous' (*Rom 5:19*).

To obey means to enter into the mystery of Christ who was *submissive* to the Father in the complexity and tragic nature of human history which he took upon himself in his life as his historic mission.

Obedience is a great mystery and cannot be simply explained by reasons to do with association or organisation. For sure, order is necessary. There is a need for someone to be in command and for there to be a chain of command: all of this is right and good, but the promise of obedience is a very profound mystery because it is about entering into the obedience of Christ to his Father. The Father has established a sacramental economy in which the divine is revealed through what is human. So, not through a direct manifestation of God alone to man alone but of God alone to man in his history.

By exploring this more in depth, it is possible to speak about *active* obedience or *passive* obedience, two terms that take our humanity in its totality and configure it to Christ.

a) *Active obedience* is the creative and responsible implementation of the Church's directives: doing what it says to do, being seriously committed to this, taking on a project to bring it to fruition in concrete circumstances.

The priest is sent to a parish to carry out the Church's directives there, and these are the directives of the Bishop, Councils, Synods, everything the tradition and discipline offer to him. However, their implementation calls for creativity and responsibility since they involve people. Very different from this is the responsibility of the official who restricts himself to blindly carrying out an order without being overly concerned about the consequences.

Priestly obedience is more delicate, more full of humanity. It is true that there will be situations where you would like to choose one solution but need, instead, to follow the opinion of the ecclesiastical authority. Nevertheless the choice always needs to be carried out in a trusting and collaborative spirit, not doing things out of spite but trying to penetrate the saving, loving intention of the one who has made the choice. The official might very well carry out his order out of spite.

Instead, the obedience that is part of the mystery of Christ's obedience is always concerned about people, the result. It might be that you suffer some inner division, but out of love and in the effort to adapt everything for the better.

The obedience that derives from reverence, then, assumes that a directive has been made, that there is a profound salvific reason for it, and, therefore, that one should try to carry it out in simplicity of heart.

A New Testament reference could be helpful for this active obedience. The Second Letter to the Corinthians comes to mind when it speaks about Paul and Titus. There were differences of opinion between the Apostle and the community: Titus is sent to Corinth to seek a reconciliation, and he carries out a form of active obedience. If he had acted purely as an official he could have run the risk of making the situation worse; instead, he showed such finesse that he rebuilt the friendship between the faithful and the Apostle. 'In addition to our own consolation, we rejoiced still more at the joy of Titus, because his mind has been set at rest by all of you. For if I have been somewhat boastful about you to him, I was not disgraced; but just as everything we said to you was true, so our boasting to Titus has proved true as well. And his heart goes out all the more to you, as he remembers the obedience of all of you, and how you welcomed him with fear and trembling. I rejoice, because I have complete confidence in you' (*2 Cor 7:13-16*). The relationship between obedience and reverence is expressed very well here. Titus obeyed and knew how to get others to obey him, and by now Paul realises he can count absolutely on the people who carry out their tasks creatively and responsibly.

b) *Passive obedience.* The term is inadequate given that the word 'passive' needs to include everything regarding the *passio Christi* that is the most redemptive and active moment of his life.

It is helpful to consider a text from the Letter to the Hebrews where we read: 'By faith Abraham obeyed when he was called to set out for a place that he was to receive as an inheritance; and he set out, not knowing where he was going' (*Heb 11:8*). Passivity is a fundamental side of obedience to the bishop and I have often heard priests, at the Silver Jubilee of ordination or parish anniversaries, recall with a great sense of inner joy: 'I came here so many years ago, sent by the Archbishop and I did not even know the name of the district; today it has become my home, my family!'

Passive obedience is going to the place where one is assigned, accepting this experience of the Church as it distributes tasks.

Humanly speaking it is not easy, because faced with a particular destination we can be fearful, even baulk at it. In these cases, I believe it is right to present your feelings and some of your desires. However, beyond this we need to be alert since we are risking wanting to make our choice and force the superiors to satisfy us. In the end we get what we want but the mission is then deprived of its strength. And then, when difficult times come, and the response is not what we hoped for and the atmosphere is heavy, we are unable to bear the situation. On the contrary, if we have obeyed passively, even when faced with adversity, we can remain at peace, knowing that since it was not us who chose this mission, the Lord will help us.

Abraham's strength was precisely in leaving out of obedience to the voice of God. Naturally, this type of obedience is exercised very rarely in life: yet it is fundamental, because it qualifies the way of being in a place and the whole attitude with which one experiences a situation. It is a bit like the choice of chastity: while being limited to certain moments, it gives shape to all the others, and embraces day and night.

While active obedience feeds off indications given and seeks to translate them into action, think about them, organise them actively, passive obedience is a privileged moment in which we can also make serious mistakes and therefore need to be helped and corrected. Chapter 12 of the Letter to the Hebrews applies in this case (*v.* 9) where it speaks about correction. Such obedience presumes differences of opinion, the possibility of criticism and strong inner resentment but this is all part of the experience of service in the Church. Naturally, this is not to say that the choice made by superiors is always the most perfect and best from a historical or objective point of view. But the Church does assure us that when we place ourselves in God's hands we do not err, because we have achieved the correct approach to life. This is the fundamental attitude included in our offer of reverence and obedience.

Finally, I would like to stress that the reverence and obedience which the deacon or priest offers the bishop is also a covenant or bilateral contract. The bishop must live in a state of reverence and obedience where the individual is concerned, God's plan in him and because of the mystery that is expressed in his vocation.

It is a bilateral contract that, while introducing the deacon or priest to a responsibility that is sometimes scary, also makes the bishop seriously responsible, involving him in the struggle with God and the angel, with the consecrated individual. Sometimes he has to oppose desires that unconsciously have aspects of pressure about them, trying to get the individual to understand that something else is good for him. Clearly, it would be very easy to satisfy someone, but the bishop must not betray the mystery of God regarding those entrusted to him.

Deacon, priest and bishop need to pray very much, contemplate, and adhere humbly to the daily demands of the Spirit, in order not to fail God's eternal plan for souls.

Pastoral charity

- How can we describe pastoral charity and what does it imply?

I will limit myself to suggesting a reflection to you that you can explore, based on the experience of Moses as Stephen interpreted it.

Moses is presented in terms of chronological events in his lifetime. Each of these stages lasts for forty years. In the first forty years he is raised and formed in Egypt and becomes 'powerful in his words and deeds' (*Acts 7:22*). In the second forty year period he throws himself into a life for his brothers and sisters of Israel and spends himself for them; then, disappointed and embittered, he takes refuge in the desert (cf. *Acts 7:23-39*). In the third forty year period Moses hears God's voice calling him and goes back to serve his brothers and sisters.

I would stress especially *verse 34* when God says: 'I have surely seen the mistreatment of my people who are in Egypt and have heard their groaning, and I have come down to rescue them. Come now, I will send you to Egypt.' This is the God who takes action because he has seen the misery of the people. He comes down and communicates with Moses that he is taking pity on Israel. This is the beginning of pastoral charity. It is not Moses' impulsive act in killing the Egyptian who was beating the Jew. That was a generous impulse, but it was not followed up, nor did the people appreciate it.

Pastoral charity begins when he receives God's communication and shares in the Lord's mercy for his people. From then on he carries out his service through difficulties, suffering and despite reaching inner limits of endurance.

Pastoral charity is not about giving up our bodies to be burned or handing over all of our goods to help the poor. Rather is it sharing in God's love placed in our hearts by the Spirit given to us (cf. *Rom 5:5*). It is sharing in the active mercy with which God has loved us, loves his people, and sees the sufferings of the people before we do, sending us to them.

In other words, it is taking up and sharing in the love with which Jesus the Good Shepherd gave his life for the flock. It is not something we win for ourselves but is a grace to ask for, a gift to receive; it is the gift of the Spirit invoked over you on the day of your ordination as deacon or priest.

Finally, I would like to remind you that the infusion of pastoral charity in the priest is not only for that moment during ordination, but is also a gradual infusion that the community pours out on the priest. The people form their priest in charity through their affection, welcome, reverence and understanding, help him grow and mature in his ability to give himself.

Concluding, let me say that the rite of ordination brings with it a sense of trepidation, emotion for the person undergoing it, a succession of different feelings, because it faces us with the seriousness of it all and makes us understand that we will confront serious and difficult situations where our whole life is at stake.

Let us ask Mary, who staked everything on her 'yes', in a radical choice that finally led her beneath the Lord's cross so as to be beside us, in order to help us experience our final moments of preparation seriously and securely.

10

STEPHEN'S PRAYER AND OUR PRAYER

In this final meditation, I propose to return to the scene of Stephen's death, the one we began our Retreat with, to reflect on the martyr's final prayer.

Let us bear in mind as a background the prayer in the ordination rite, the prayer of consecration: 'Lord, send forth upon him the Holy Spirit, that he may be strengthened by the gift of your sevenfold grace to carry out faithfully the work of the ministry.'

Let us read the text of Chapter 7 of Acts where it says: 'But filled with the Holy Spirit, he gazed into heaven and saw the glory of God and Jesus standing at the right hand of God. "Look," he said, " see the heavens opened and the Son of Man standing at the right hand of God!" But they covered their ears, and with a loud shout all rushed together against him. Then they dragged him out of the city and began to stone him; and the witnesses laid their coats at the feet of a young man named Saul. While they were stoning Stephen, he prayed, "Lord Jesus, receive my spirit." Then he knelt down and cried out in a loud voice, "Lord, do not hold this sin against them." When he had said this, he died' (*Acts 7:55-60*).

We can ask ourselves:

– who is praying?
– what is the situation in which he is praying?
– what is he asking?

Who is praying?

1. The subject of the prayer is clearly the *man filled with the Holy Spirit*.

We have seen that this fullness, indicated as being a characteristic of Stephen's final moment, had already been anticipated in him through similar expressions, both with regard to the choice of the seven and in reference to him as a person. He had been called full of wisdom, faith, grace, power: four characteristics – *sophìa, pìstis, chàris, dynamis* – which are added together and sometimes interwoven, to underline Stephen's growth in his mission (cf. *Acts 6:3,5,8*).

What do these four terms point to?

– Taking the term *wisdom* as the result of the entire Old Testament reflection of wise men as far as the wisdom of the perfect ones in the First Letter to the Corinthians, we can describe it as the gift of those who can perceive God's presence within the framework of the historical journey of humanity.

Wisdom is the gift of the Spirit who permits human beings to establish their coordinates in history based not simply on facts and data but on contemplation of the entire picture, so they can grasp its meaning in relationship to God's call and plan.

The wise person is the one who understands human history as being part of the plan of salvation; such a lofty gift corresponds to a particular grace that is given even to very simple folk.

– Stephen's *faith*, located within a context of miracles, healings, extraordinary works, is not directly theological faith but practical faith, the kind I have when I have the strong feeling that God, in a specific situation in life, is working powerfully through me. It is the grace that the people of Nazareth did not have (cf. *Mk 6:1-6*): they believed in God but did not believe that his love was at work among them in that situation. So they lacked the ability to sense that the Lord loves them *here* and *now* and lacked a practical trust in him in the immediate circumstances of their life.

Instead, the gift of Stephen's faith consisted in the certainty that despite his unworthiness, God was acting through his hands, through his prayer, and his anointing of the sick.

– To this is added *grace* (*chàris*) which translates the Old Testament reality known as divine *hésed*, the merciful grace of the covenant. Stephen experiences his possibility of helping not as self-sufficiency but as the gift of God who showed mercy to him and will therefore show mercy to others.

– Grace is expressed in *power* (*dynamis*), the practicality of taking action, doing, speaking.

These are four characteristics that, taken as a whole, offer us the figure of a servant of the brethren in body and spirit, enlightened, ardent, effective, trusting but also humble, not at all boastful, not puffed up but calmly abandoned to divine action.

To better understand this fullness of Stephen's we can compare it with Mary's fullness when she is told: 'The Holy Spirit will come upon you, and the power [*dynamis*, energy] of the Most High will overshadow you' (*Lk 1:35*). Here, it does not speak of fullness but of being overshadowed by, immersed in the glorious cloud that represents the overpowering strength of God active in history and in her life. The Virgin knows that all this is gift, and exclaims: 'My soul magnifies the Lord ... For the Mighty One has done great things for me ... He has shown *strength* [practical energy] with his arm' (*Lk 1:46*).

2. Fullness of the Spirit is also asked for in the prayer over the ordinands. There are three features of this very brief formula I would like to stress:

– Since it is a prayer, the bishop limits himself to *interceding*. It is not the power of human action that is manifested but the weakness of intercession. Not all the sacramental formulas are prayer in this sense. For example, in the formula of absolution in the sacrament of Penance, it is a fact that is expressed, a reality in which the Church reconciles by virtue of its powers.

Here, instead, there is an appeal to divine power and for our part there is a need for faith, abandonment and acceptance.

– It is a prayer that has the *Spirit* as its direct object: 'Send forth upon him the Holy Spirit.' It is modelled directly on what happened to Mary. The fullness of divine power is invoked, not just some special gift.

– It is invoked 'that he may be strengthened by the gift of your sevenfold grace to carry out faithfully the work of the *ministry*'.

The fullness of the Spirit is in view of ministerial fulfilment, a service carried out through the bestowal of a rainbow's worth of gifts, the entire gamut of sensitivities and spiritual powers that express it. And it needs to be received as such.

The specific features of the service, therefore, derive from the richness of inner abundance, of creativity, joy, happiness, serenity, fluency, spontaneous ability, which the Spirit evokes.

In what situation does Stephen pray?

1. We have already said that Stephen is praying at the most serious moment of his existence: his prayer is an expression of existential clarity, now no longer veiled and where there is no possibility of misunderstanding.

2. What is the situation in which the prayer over the ordinands is said? It is one of relative existential clarity because it comes at the end of a period of formation,

reflection on oneself, one's character, a certain self-evaluation and knowledge of life and reality.

It also finds the ordinand at a highly responsible moment. In fact, you know that in the current discipline granting dispensation from the obligations of celibacy and the priestly state, the fundamental question is as follows: in what situation did the conferring of Orders take place?

If it can be demonstrated that it took place in a situation where there was no existential clarity, it is possible for the dispensation to be granted. If, on the contrary, there is no doubt about the clarity of the situation, the current discipline does not grant dispensation.

So, existential clarity is the source of great responsibility, because it places us in the adult situation of taking on definitive roles and tasks.

Naturally, such clarity involves both the ordinands and those ordaining, the local Church, those who do the laying on of hands. They too take on a serious responsibility that commits them throughout their life to supporting, promoting and protecting this gift of God.

What does Stephen ask for?

Stephen addresses two very intense, affectionate prayers to the Lord Jesus. They point to a profound familiarity with Christ, a profound interpersonal relationship. I believe we could say that they are the first prayers addressed to him by a Christian who was not an original disciple of Jesus. It is true that the Emmaus disciples turned to their Master in prayer, but this was still a prayer spoken in darkness. Stephen is the first to do so in the full clarity of the resurrection.

– 'Lord Jesus, receive my spirit' (*Acts 7:59*). The object of this prayer concerns himself, and basically it wants to say: Lord, I give you my life, I offer myself. There is an attitude of humility in the fact that Stephen asks to be received. The offering is implied in the action that he fulfils.

He asks to be received with that fullness of gift with which God created and recreated him. It is the prayer of Jesus on the cross: 'Father, into your hands I commend my spirit' (*Lk 23:46*) and John, in his Gospel, interprets it in the sense that Jesus gives back the Spirit to the Father and does so for humankind.

– 'Lord, do not hold this sin against them' (*Acts 7:60*). Stephen's second prayer concerns the others, and it too is sublime, because it does not come from any simple human reflection but from the situation where he identifies himself with Jesus crucified. It comes from intense contemplation of the cross. We recall that St Charles Borromeo spent a long time in contemplation of the cross, that was for him the inspiration for every action and decision.

Stephen had contemplated the death of Christ at length and had profoundly entered into identity of feeling with the heart of Jesus, so he could say to the Father with him: do not look to me but to them, do not be concerned about me but about them, be concerned with their weakness, poverty, have mercy on them and forgive them, accept my life for them.

The two prayers, so brief yet so moving, genuine, transparent, are basically *the prayer of pastoral charity* that concerns self and others, concerns ourselves and those around us, and its culminating moment comes with the offering of ourselves.

We need to constantly ask for the gift of this apostolic prayer. We are not asked to make a great effort at identification (that could be an unrealistic stretch of the imagination), but to say: *Lord, I recognise that I am far from Stephen's attitude; I admire him because it was your prayer on the cross and I beg that you grant me the gift of the Spirit that will lead me where you want me to go, and will keep me on this path and lead me to the situation you have prepared for me.*

Let us pray, today and in the days to come, for one another, in the knowledge that a priest achieves the maturity of Christian contemplation when he receives the gift of the prayer of pastoral charity.

CARLO MARIA MARTINI Foundation

The Carlo Maria Martini Foundation came into existence through the initiative of the Italian Province of the Jesuits and with the involvement of the Archdiocese of Milan.

It aims at remembering Cardinal Carlo Maria Martini by promoting knowledge and study of his life and works and keeping alive the spirit that animated his commitment, encouraging experience and knowledge of the Word of God in the context of our contemporary culture.

With this in mind, the Foundation's role is spelt out in a number of specific actions:

- Bringing the Cardinal's works, writings and addresses together in an archive and promoting their study as well as encouraging and authorising their publication.
- Supporting and nurturing ecumenical and inter-religious dialogue, with civil society and non-believers as well, working closely together to understand the indissoluble connection between faith, justice and culture.
- Fostering the study of Scripture involving other disciplines, including spirituality and social sciences.
- Contributing to pastoral and formative projects valuing Ignatian pedagogy and addressed especially to the young.
- Supporting study of the meaning and extended practice of the Spiritual Exercises.

Those who wish to can contribute to the collection of materials (written, audio, video) on Cardinal Martini by indicating initiatives regarding him by writing to segretaria@fondazionecarlomariamartini.it

To subscribe to the newsletter (in Italian) and support the Foundation's activities: www.fondazionecarlomariamartini.it

BIBLICAL MEDITATIONS

A selection of sermons, retreats and meditation texts drawn from the vast work of Cardinal Martini. There is a roundup of biblical personalities from Old and New Testaments, explanations, some chosen topics to accompany reflections on the human being in search of God. The inestimable legacy of a man of prayer and contemporary spirituality.

1. **The Accounts of the Passion.** Meditations
2. **Paul.** In the thick of his ministry
3. **Our Father.** Do not heap up empty phrases
4. **The Apostles.** Men of peace and reconciliation
5. **Abraham.** Our father in faith
6. **Jesus.** Why he spoke in parables?
7. **Elijah.** The living God
8. **Stephen.** Servant and witness
9. **Peter.** Confessions
10. **Jacob.** A man's dream
11. **Jeremiah.** A prophetic voice in the city
12. **Israel.** A people on the move
13. **Samuel.** Religious and civil prophet
14. **Timothy.** Timothy's way

www.ingramcontent.com/pod-product-compliance
Lightning Source LLC
Chambersburg PA
CBHW030635150426
428IICB000778/2117/J